D1605290

THE 25 GREATEST MOMENTS IN
LAMBEAU FIELD HISTORY

BY CLIFF CHRISTL AND DALE HOFMANN

KCI SPORTS

CREDITS

ISBN: 0-9798729-0-1
ISBN 13: 978-09798729-0-7

This book is available in quantity at special discounts for your group or organization. For further information, contact:

KCI Sports Publishing
3340 Whiting Avenue
Suite 5
Stevens Point, WI 54481
(217) 766-3390
Fax: (715) 344-2668

Publisher: Peter J. Clark
Managing Editor: Molly Voorheis
Cover Design: Nicky Brillowski
Book Layout and Design: Nicky Brillowski
Sales & Marketing: Dirk Sorenson

Printed in the United States

CONTENTS

ACKNOWLEGDEMENT

Thanks to the more than 35 former and current players, as well as former general manager Ron Wolf, who shared their time and memories with us. Also thanks to Mark Schiefelbein, Jeff Blumb and others in the Packers' organization who offered assistance in setting up some of the interviews. A special thanks to Bob Harlan and Larry McCarren for writing forewords for the book. Last but not least, thanks to Peter Clark of KCI Sports for recruiting us to write the book and overseeing the project.

DEDICATION

To my mother Jane K. Sapiro, who passed on to me her high standards of integrity and nose for news; to my late father Clifford H. Christl, who died when I was 13 days old after serving his country with honor and distinction in World War II and fighting in the Battle of the Bulge; and to my late maternal grandmother Lillian Hansen, who passed on to me her interest in history and offered me use of her typewriter at a young age. Also to my wife and best friend, Shirley Christl; daughters Kelly Christl and Cassie Christl Schmitt, and stepsons Keith, Ryan and Brandon Fabry, and all of their families. That includes grandson Isaac Schmitt, already a big football fan at age 3.

Cliff Christl

To Sandy, my wife, friend, teacher, sounding board, copy editor and confidante, the one who makes everything possible. To Tara, Dana, Kyle and Maren, who grew up quietly and well while Dad warred with the keyboard. And to Paul Ludlam, the bravest man I've ever known.

Dale Hofmann

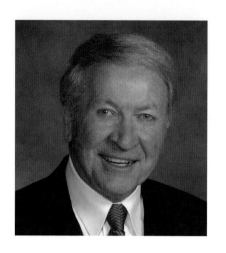

FOREWORD

BOB HARLAN
CHAIRMAN OF THE BOARD
& CEO GREEN BAY PACKERS

Every once in a while when I need to get away for a little bit, I'll come down from my office and take a walk through the tunnel at Lambeau Field and stand in the south end zone. I like to go late in the day when the sun's going down and the stadium is really quiet. The quietness appeals to me. I'll just think of all of the things that have happened on that field, of the players, the coaches, the games, of how raucous it can be. And how very peaceful it can be late in the afternoon. I guess you could say it's my Field of Dreams. Going down there is a getaway for me. I don't do it every day, but I do it often. Lambeau is such a great place.

It has a history, a tradition and an intimacy that makes it so different from any other stadium in the league. There is just a mystique about it. There aren't many historic stadiums left anymore, but this is definitely one of them. You really have only Wrigley Field, Fenway Park, Yankee Stadium and Lambeau Field now, and Yankee Stadium is going to be changed very soon.

To be able to tell people that the Lombardi teams practiced and played at Lambeau and that the Holmgren Super Bowl teams practiced and played there as well was a huge advantage when we were campaigning for the renovation referendum that would save the Green Bay Packers franchise.

The first thing we had to find out was whether the stadium bowl was good enough for us to preserve the facility. The bowl was 43 years old at the time, and I wanted to know if it was sturdy enough to last another 30 or 35 years. The experts ran it through every test possible, and they came back and said it absolutely was. That was the whole key to keeping the stadium that has meant so much to the Green Bay Packers.

My best memory at Lambeau Field came on January 12, 1997, when we beat Carolina to win the NFC championship. I will never forget that day.

Ron Wolf and I went down to the north end zone with about two minutes to go in the game to receive the trophy from Chicago Bears owner Virginia McCaskey, the daughter of the late George Halas. When the game ended, the first thing the public address announcer said was, "Ladies and gentlemen, the Green Bay Packers are going to the Super Bowl." And then they played "We Are the Champions." The players were jumping around and throwing their helmets in the air, but it was watching the fans that really got to me.

There was such joy in that stadium. Every place I looked, I could see people hugging and high-fiving. We'd given out towels before the game, and when I looked up to the private boxes and the club seats, I could see the people there waving the towels and jumping up and down.

I thought, "Who deserves this more than these fans?" They had hung with us so loyally in the '70s and '80s when we'd had only four winning seasons, and I think many of them believed that this could never happen again in Green Bay. But here we were, going to the Super Bowl again.

Just to hear those words "going to the Super Bowl" over the PA had an enormous effect on me. I was very emotional standing on that field, and then when I got to the locker room about an hour later and I was trying to tell members of the media what a great experience it was, I actually broke up.

I've talked to so many people who were in the stands who have told me they cried that day because they were so happy. I don't know if we'll ever see that kind of happiness again. I mean, winning the Super Bowl was the ultimate accomplishment, but to win that big game here at Lambeau Field was my fondest memory.

It was a very cold day, but nobody wanted to leave the stadium after the game. Everyone just wanted to cherish the moment. That scene would be tough for me to top because it happened here. I love this stadium as much as I love the franchise.

FOREWORD

LARRY McCARREN
MEMBER OF GREEN BAY PACKERS HALL OF FAME
CURRENT COLOR COMMENTATOR - PACKERS
RADIO NETWORK

God bless Cliff Christl and Dale Hofmann. Narrowing the greatest moments at Lambeau Field to "the" 25 greatest, and then ranking them — that is a task worthy of divine intervention. The best of Lambeau Field is much of the NFL's best. Fifty years worth of great games, all the plays and all the players, there's just so much rich history to choose from.

My first great Lambeau Field moment came as a high school kid growing up in suburban Chicago. I watched the Ice Bowl at a friend's house. (Rich kid — had a TV in his room). I'm sure I had seen other games broadcast from Lambeau but that is truly the first one I remember, and how could it ever be forgotten? It was everything football was supposed to be: Overcoming not only an opponent, but the elements as well, and doing it under the pressure of an unbiased clock. Little did I know that one day I would actually have the privilege of playing on that same frozen tundra.

My greatest moment at Lambeau Field as a player came on October 17, 1983. That's when we beat the defending Super Bowl champion Washington Redskins 48-47 on Monday Night Football. It is still the highest scoring game in MNF history. We had a home run offense that season, and we hit a bunch of them that night. And thank you, Mark Moseley for missing that last-second field goal. I can still see our offensive coordinator, Bob Schnelker, turning his back to the field. He couldn't bear to watch the kick that would have made it a great moment in Redskin history.

I've also had the good fortune to witness more than a few great moments in my current role of broadcaster, and my all-time favorite was the NFC championship game played on January 12, 1997. The Packers whipped the Carolina Panthers 30-13 and earned the right to play in Super Bowl XXXI. It was official, the Pack was Back, and seeing the genuine happiness of all concerned — the players, the coaches, Bob Harlan and Ron Wolf, and of course the fans — that's what made it so great. I can't remember a single play from the game, but I can remember a real warm feeling at Lambeau on a bitterly cold day.

Those three games are so special that they'd make almost anyone's list of the Greatest Moments at Lambeau Field, but I'm sure we all could put together a more personal edition. Mine would include being part of the halftime ceremonies in which Reggie White's number 92 was retired, a much forgotten playoff game where we beat the then St. Louis Cardinals 41-16 and of course the "Chester Marcol" game that opened the '80 season. It made "the" Top 25 because he won it by scooping up a blocked field goal and running it in for the winning touchdown in overtime. It makes my list because I was recovering from hernia surgery and was happy the damn thing was finally over. As a matter of fact, I think I was a major contributor to the blocked field goal.

I trust you'll enjoy *The 25 Greatest Moments in Lambeau Field History*. Nobody can turn a phrase like Dale Hofmann, and if Cliff Christl's involved, it's accurate, thorough and well-researched. But trust me on this- their list isn't the only list. Perhaps your list would include the first time you went to Lambeau with your dad, or that time you took your son or daughter to see the Packers play. Maybe you were on the receiving end of a Lambeau Leap. It doesn't have to involve a great game to qualify as a great moment. Packers fans, just by being Packers fans, have made for many, many great moments at Lambeau Field. They've made the team and its home part of the fabric of the community, and their passion is palpable. You can feel their energy on the field, and that, in and of itself, is always a great moment.

Enjoy.

INTRODUCTION

Lambeau Field has been home to the Green Bay Packers for 50 years, making it the longest serving stadium to a single franchise since the National Football League came into being in 1920. That fact alone all but tells you that Lambeau has been the site of not only many of the greatest moments in the Packers' storied history, but also in NFL history.

In fact, it's worth asking: In what other stadium has more of the league's history been written?

When Lambeau — or new City Stadium as it was then called — was dedicated on Sept. 29, 1957, former commissioner Bert Bell gushed that it was "the greatest thing that has ever happened in professional football." Fifty years later, Lambeau, the first stadium in the country built exclusively for a pro football franchise, has become widely recognized as not just a stadium, but a shrine to the game itself.

Thanks to a $295 million redevelopment project and two large bronze statues of Curly Lambeau and Vince Lombardi that stand in front of the main gate, Lambeau Field has only recently taken on a majestic look on the outside. Inside, the Lambeau bowl has always portrayed a simple elegance that honors football's past and has always created an intimate setting to celebrate the present.

That's all part of an atmosphere that makes a great game at Lambeau even more special and made our task of picking the 25 best even more difficult.

In Lambeau's first 50 seasons, the Packers played 233 regular-season and 14 playoff games there. Twelve of the 21 Packers who have been inducted into the Pro Football Hall of Fame played in Lambeau and another coached there.

In the early years of the stadium, the Packers forged one of the great dynasties in pro football history under that Hall of Fame coach, Vince Lombardi. More recently, during the career of future Hall of Famer Brett Favre, the Packers achieved one of the most successful runs in pro football history by going 13 straight seasons without a losing record.

So where does one start in picking out the 25 greatest moments or games?

We based our choices on three criteria and, for the most part, applied equal weight to each.

1)   The stakes.
2)   Historical significance.
3)   The story lines.

To backtrack for a moment, we chose only games that were won by the Packers. For example, the Chicago Bears stunned the Packers, 10-3, in the 1963 season opener. It was a victory that propelled the Bears to the NFL title that year and might be regarded as one of the great games in Bears history. But this book was written for an audience largely of Packer fans and, thus, the games were selected with that in mind.

But back to our three criteria.

Clearly, the bigger the game the more important it was at the time. The biggest games in Lambeau's history were the two NFL championships played there in 1961 and '65 in the pre-Super Bowl era. Lambeau also served as host to another NFL championship in 1967 prior to Super Bowl II, but also before the NFL-AFL merger was completely implemented. Since the merger was completed in 1970, the Packers also have played one NFC championship at Lambeau and that against Carolina prior to their winning Super Bowl XXXI.

All four of those NFL or NFC championship games are among our top 10 games.

At the same time, we determined that not every playoff game was a top 25 moment. One other that we included was the 1965 Western Conference playoff against Baltimore that went into overtime back when only two teams made the playoffs unless there was a tie in the final standings as there was that year. We also included one of two divisional playoff games — those played on the second week of the playoffs under the current format — and two of seven wild card or first-round playoff games.

The 1996 divisional playoff against San Francisco made it; the 1997, 21-7 divisional playoff victory over Tampa Bay didn't.

The two wild card games chosen were the victory over Detroit in 1994 when the Packers held the great Barry Sanders to minus-one yard rushing and the victory over Seattle following the 2003 season that was won on a defensive touchdown in overtime by Al Harris.

A first-round playoff victory over St. Louis following the strike-shortened 1982 season; and wild card victories over Atlanta in 1995 and San Francisco following the '01 season were not included. The Packers also lost two wild card games at home.

Among the regular-season games on the list were a huge victory over another powerhouse, Detroit, early in the Packers' 1962 championship run; another pivotal victory over the Lions that helped secure a Central Division title in 1972; a momentum shifting, late-season victory over the Bears in 1995; a division-clinching victory over Pittsburgh in '95 that ended a 23-year drought; and an overtime victory over San Francisco in 1996 that ultimately decided home field advantage for the playoffs.

It is worth noting here that the Packers played only two home games in December and never clinched a conference or division title at home during Lombardi's nine years. That partly explains why there weren't more regular-season showdowns on the list.

In gauging historical significance, there couldn't help but be some overlap with the first criterion. Again, the bigger the game the more likely it was to be historically important. But we also viewed historical significance through a different lens than just the stakes that were involved.

For example, the 1961 NFL championship against the New York Giants seemed bigger at the time than the 1967 NFL title game against Dallas. The '61 championship was the first ever played in Green Bay and was more eagerly anticipated and led to a more wild and spontaneous celebration. But the '67 game, famously referred to as the Ice Bowl, became Lambeau Field's defining game as the stadium's tradition grew over time, not to mention it was much closer and produced far more drama.

Other games that warranted a high grade for historical significance included the Dedication Game in 1957; Lombardi's first game in 1959; Paul Hornung's club-record, 33-point game against Baltimore in 1961; the first Monday night game against New England in 1979; Favre's Lambeau debut against Cincinnati in 1992; Reggie White's coming out party against Denver in 1993; and the game against the Los Angeles Raiders in 1993 when LeRoy Butler introduced the "Lambeau Leap."

And, again, some of those games look bigger today through the lens of history than they did at the time. When Butler leaped into the stands following his touchdown against the Raiders, it was hardly noted in the next day's game accounts. But some 13 years later, the "Lambeau Leap" has come to symbolize the bond between Packer fans and their team.

In turn, the Packers' victory over Seattle on Harris' interception in a wild card playoff game provided one of the most dramatic finishes in the history of Lambeau, but that game lost much of its historical significance when the

Packers were bounced from the playoffs the next week in Philadelphia.

Then again, there was more to that Seattle game than just the playoff consequences. It also marked another return to Lambeau by Mike Holmgren and the rest of the entourage that he took to Seattle and was spiced by Matt Hasselbeck's guarantee following the coin flip before overtime.

That was all part of the story line, our third criterion. To be sure, there's more overlap here. If it's a big game or a historically significant game that's part of the story line. But drama, any bizarre development and so much more can also be part of a game's story line.

The Packers' 48-47 victory over Washington in 1983 was the highest scoring game in Packers history and the highest scoring game ever on Monday night television, and it ended with an unexpected finish on the game's final play. The game had no bearing on the playoff race that year — the Packers were en route to an 8-8 finish — but it certainly provided one of the best story lines in Packers history.

The same could be said for the Packers' fluke victory over the Bears on kicker Chester Marcol's touchdown in overtime in 1980; the Snow Bowl against Tampa Bay in 1985; the Instant Replay game, another last-minute victory over the Bears, in 1989; and the Packers' Monday night, overtime victory over Minnesota on Antonio Freeman's improbable catch in 2000.

We understand our list is open to argument. We'll even admit that if somebody asked us today to compile a new list and we weren't allowed to refresh our memories with this book, we might even come up with a different order.

There were games that we regretted leaving off: The Packers' narrow victory over the 49ers in 1959 that left them as the only unbeaten team in the league a season after they had finished 1-10-1 under Scooter McLean; their 49-0 thrashing of the Bears in 1962; the '82 playoff against St. Louis; the Packers' victory over New Orleans in 1989 after being down 21-0 at halftime; their victory over Dallas, snapping an eight-game losing streak to the Cowboys, in 1997; any of the three down-to-the-wire victories produced by Favre over three straight home games in 1999; and the Packers' stunning offensive outburst against the defending Super Bowl champion Baltimore Ravens in 2001.

But that was to be expected.

What makes Lambeau so sacred also makes this list less than sacred. With a stadium so rich in history, it's a tall order to pick the best of anything.

All we can claim is that we had a formula and we tried our best.

14

Opposite page: John
Brockington pounds his way
through the Detroit defense.
Brockington gained 86 yards
on 25 carries and scored
twice as the Packers gained
the inside track on their first
division title in five years.

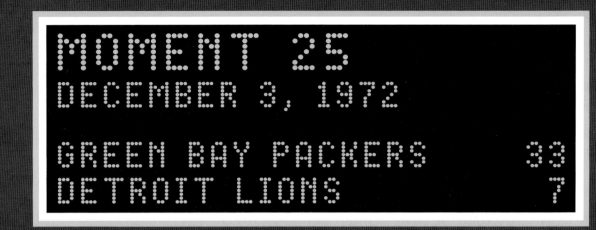

MOMENT 25
DECEMBER 3, 1972

GREEN BAY PACKERS   33
DETROIT LIONS   7

BROKEN PROMISES

Everything looked so bright when the one-armed cornerback came up with his second interception. Jim Carter tipped Greg Landry's pass at the 50, and Kenny Ellis plucked it out of the air and ran to the Detroit 10. Two plays later, John Brockington scored, giving the Packers a 30-0 lead and a straight path to their first division championship in five years.

How fitting that Ellis should be the star of the game. A week earlier, he had his right shoulder dislocated while making a fair catch against the Washington Redskins. The doctors were telling him that he was done for the season. It turned out he wasn't even done for the week. With his shoulder taped and wrapped in a harness, he set up touchdowns with both of his picks and rounded out his day by recovering a fumble.

A most unlikely hero on an incredibly unlikely team.

By drilling the Lions that day, the Packers opened a one-game lead in the NFC Central. The next week they trounced the Minnesota Vikings, 23-7, and ended a championship drought that had started right after the Ice Bowl. A young group with a second-year quarterback, a second-year coach, a dominant defense and a killer running game, the '72 Packers seemed poised for another long, prosperous run. Three weeks later, their future was behind them.

Washington would beat them badly in the NFC divisional playoff on Christmas Eve, and the Packers would not win another division title for 23 years. In fact, they would have only one winning season in the next nine as dissension and disappointment wracked the franchise. And it all started with the mind-bending anomalies on this incredibly contradictory team.

The second-year quarterback was Scott Hunter, who had come to the Packers as a sixth-round draft choice from Alabama. Hunter had made an assault on Joe Namath's records with the Crimson Tide, but he completed only 86 passes for the Packers in 1972. The previous season he'd completed 75, the fewest of any Green Bay starting quarterback since 1959.

Hunter's leading targets were MacArthur Lane, his halfback, and John Brockington, his fullback. No wide receiver on the roster caught more than 16 passes. Tight end Rich McGeorge, whom Hunter claimed would have been good for at least 35 catches, missed all but two games with a knee injury. Gale Gillingham, the team's best offensive lineman, had been switched to defense where he also hurt his knee and missed the final 12 games. Hunter completed only 43.2% of his passes with nine interceptions and only six touchdowns as the Packers finished 22nd in the league in total offense. And still they won the division with a 10-4 record.

The dominating defense, ranked second in the NFL, included all-pro Ken Ellis, Pro Bowl players Bob Brown and Fred Carr as well as three-time former Pro Bowler Dave Robinson and NFL Defensive Rookie of the Year Willie Buchanan. In the center of it was middle linebacker Carter, a strong and quick third-year man from Minnesota whose relationship with the fans was never anything but rocky. They never forgave him for supplanting Ray Nitschke in the starting lineup.

Robinson would be traded, and Brown would essentially eat himself out of a job the following year. Buchanan shattered his leg that same season and was never the same again.

The killer running game was led by Brockington, who rushed for 1,027 yards, and by Lane, who contributed 821 yards and never had any trouble with the public, although he had come in a trade for the popular Donny Anderson. The following year, Brockington became

Although he might not have been popular with his players, Dan Devine was riding high when he led the Packers to the NFC Central Division title in 1972. But two years later, "Can Dan!" was a popular bumper sticker in Green Bay.

the first NFL running back to gain 1,000 yards in each of his first three seasons. He stayed four more seasons but never gained 1,000 again.

And then there was the second-year coach. The Packers Executive Committee had reluctantly hired Dan Devine in 1971. The vote was 5-2. A legend at the University of Missouri, he took a 6-8 team and led it to a 4-8-2 record his first year. His staff was divided between the people he brought in and the Vince Lombardi-era holdovers he inherited, and the division grew even as the team prospered.

He was named the NFC Coach of the Year in 1972, leading a club that prided itself on togetherness even as some of the players were saying that they were winning in spite of him. Come 1974, he was on his way to Notre Dame, trading one storied tradition for another.

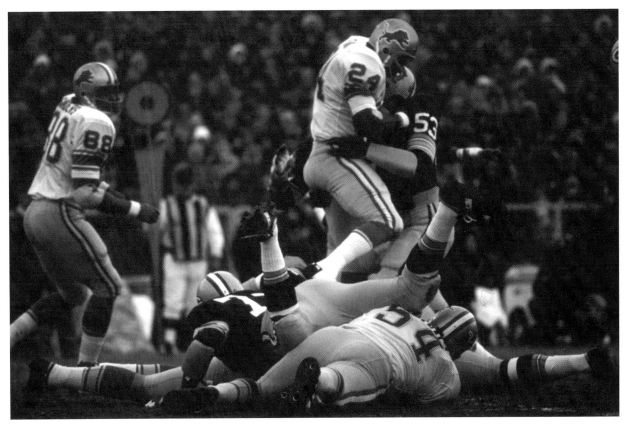

Linebacker Fred Carr stuffs the Lions' Mel Farr. Detroit was held to 27 yards rushing.

"He hated Lombardi. It ticked him off that anybody revered Lombardi," Robinson said. "He said more than once, 'I'm tired of all these Lombardi people.' After the season, he cleaned house of all the Lombardi people. He said he didn't like veterans, meaning Lombardi people."

Robinson claims that at one point Devine told the team that he had given up on it, and he was turning it over to his assistants until he could get his own players the following season. Then, Robinson said, the Packers made the playoffs, and he wanted to be the coach again. Robinson didn't get much corroboration on that, but it was clear that Devine wasn't the most popular man in the locker room.

"I guess because we knew not many people were favorable of the coach, we came together as a team," Ellis said. "In spite of him, we knew what we had. As a secondary, we were such a close-knit group of guys. I remember the next season when my wife had our second child, Willie Buchanan, Jim Hill, Al Matthews and I were at the movies together. I got the call that my wife was going into labor, so we all left the movies and took her to the hospital. That's the kind of camaraderie we had as a team.

"Devine wanted the credit for everything. He was just stuck on himself. He wasn't truthful with some players about some things. We weren't playing for Coach Devine. We were playing for each other. We were playing for the Green Bay Packers."

Whoever they were playing for, they were playing well as they entered the crucial match-up with Detroit. In fact, Lee Remmel, the team historian, said he thought the '72 Packers were playing as well as any Green Bay team in history down the stretch. After losing two games in a row against Atlanta and Minnesota, they'd won six out of seven, and while they weren't scoring a lot of touchdowns, they were getting plenty of field goals from Chester Marcol. A second-round draft choice from Hillsdale College, Marcol would lead the league in scoring as a rookie.

Hunter says that his kicker's success had a lot to do with how he and quarterback coach Bart Starr approached the game.

"The goal posts were on the goal line then, so when I got inside the 25-yard line with Chester Marcol, I'm thinking 'three' unless you have to score a touchdown," Hunter said. "Remember, we had a good defense, too, and we could eat up the clock. I didn't have the greatest passing statistics, but a lot of that was what I was thinking and what Bart was thinking. Inside the 25-yard line we had a sure three points, so I didn't do a lot of things I

had done in college, like throw the ball in the end zone on a jump ball."

Marcol was his normal productive self again that day with four field goals ranging from 24 yards to 42, although he did miss a 42-yarder and he had one blocked from 41. But he gave the Packers a 9-0 first quarter lead, and they added a couple of second quarter touchdowns on a one-yard Brockington plunge and a nine-yard scramble by Hunter to go into the intermission with a 23-0 lead.

The Lions gained only 26 yards in the first half, and anything the Green Bay defense didn't do to them, the weather did. It was 10 degrees at kickoff with a wind chill factor of minus-10. The electric blanket under the field had been on all week, and while that kept the turf warm, it didn't do much for the players.

"On the opening drive, we kept it like 17 plays and 9 minutes on the clock, which is about 15 or 20 minutes real time," said Hunter. "We took the lead on a field goal, but I was disappointed that we didn't score a touchdown. As I was trotting off the field and Chester was trotting on, I noticed all the Lion offensive guys just stomping their feet, trying to warm themselves up, rubbing themselves and gathered around the heaters. I said to myself, 'We've got these guys.' And we just killed them. Instead of melting down, they froze up."

Meanwhile, the Packers were warming to the task. The Lions ran only three plays in the first quarter, and the second quarter was no improvement as Landry threw his first interception to Ellis, and the Packers capitalized on it with Brockington's first touchdown. When Ellis made his second pick on the third play of the second half, the

Lions were done. "I thought I was going to get it in the end zone,"Ellis said.

Not that it mattered. Brockington scored again on an 8-yard run two plays later, and the only disappointment the Packers would suffer was losing the shutout when Detroit scored with 3 seconds left. The rest was all good for Green Bay. Its offense had amassed 310 yards and scored seven times, its defense had limited the Lions to 189 yards and created six turnovers, and its special teams had produced 12 points.

And the coaching? Well, when Hunter was asked what role Devine had in the victory, he said, "He was there."

Defensive tackle Mike McCoy was much more charitable. "It might have been a plan of his to get us so mad at him that we bonded together as a team because we were so young," he said. "Maybe he wanted us to take all of our frustrations out on him, and the assistant coaches could be the good guys while he was the bad guy. I thought about that many times."

It's a theory that never really got tested. Two years later, Devine was gone. But the frustrations stayed around much longer than that.

Quarterback Scott Hunter follows through on one of his 13 passes. The Packers gained only 76 yards passing, but rushed for 234.

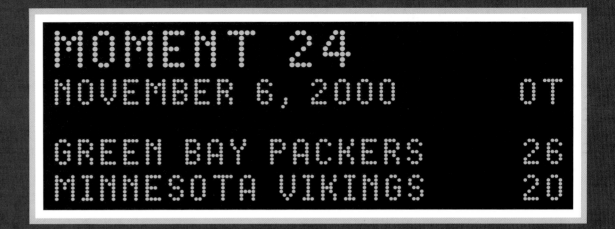

Opposite page: Brett Favre makes a last second adjustment at the line of scrimmage before throwing his dramatic touchdown pass to Antonio Freeman in a Monday night game for the ages.

MOMENT 24
NOVEMBER 6, 2000   OT

GREEN BAY PACKERS   26
MINNESOTA VIKINGS   20

BACK AT YOU

Antonio Freeman was flat on his back, and so were the Green Bay Packers. They had lost three of their last four starts, they trailed Minnesota in the NFC Central by four games, and Brett Favre had just thrown a pass in the direction of a Vikings cornerback in overtime.

Five Minnesota turnovers had kept Green Bay in a game it had to win on a sloppy Monday night marked by intermittent drizzle and winds gusting to 25 mph. Only the elements had saved the Packers from dropping to 3-6 on the season when Mitch Berger bobbled the snap for what would have been a game-winning 33-yard field goal with 7 seconds left in regulation. A national television audience and a strangely bi-partisan crowd of 59,854 knew they were lucky to be alive.

The Vikings had been making mistakes all night, and that included the coin flip. They called tails, it came up heads, and the Packers got the ball first in overtime. Six plays later, they had a third down with four yards to go on the Minnesota 43. As the teams lined up, Freeman and Brett Favre had a meeting of the minds.

"We got to the line of scrimmage, and the Vikings looked like they were in an all-out blitz," Freeman recalled. "That made the corners come up in bump and run coverage, and the safeties came down as well. So I immediately looked at Brett to try to alert him, but he took a few steps to alert me, and we looked at each other and gave each other the same exact signal, which was a slant and go. It was a perfect play because once you run the slant, there's nobody behind.

"But then I think the ball must have gotten wet, or the wind might have blown it, because the referee came in and replaced it. When he did that, the Vikings adjusted their defense and backed out of the bump and run. Our offenses were so similar that I'm sure when I gave the signal and Brett gave it back, they knew. They immediately started the play clock, and we didn't have a lot of time. We had to stay with the play we called. We decided, let's go with it anyway, put it up in the air and give me a chance."

From Favre's point of view, it was the only decision. As he explained it after the game, "Hey, when your star player wants the ball, give it to him."

Freeman appreciated the sentiment, especially since he was hardly getting star treatment at the time. He had signed a six-year, $42 million contract a year and a half earlier after catching a career-high 84 passes for 1,424 yards and 14 touchdowns in 1998, but his numbers had fallen in 1999, and they were slipping again in 2000. Not only was he feeling underused, he was $9,000 poorer after Mike Sherman fined him for coming back late from the bye a couple of weeks earlier.

Freeman's best years had been under Mike Holmgren, the undisputed master of the short passing game, but when Ray Rhodes replaced Holmgren, Freeman said the team's offensive philosophy changed. Then Sherman replaced Rhodes and made the changes permanent.

"It was a tough time for me," Freeman said. "I had to hold out for a contract, and a lot of people were saying, 'I hope he's worth the money. I hope he does this. I hope he does that.' All of the weight shifted to my shoulders, like there weren't 21 other people who had to play offense and defense. In that regard, I had a lot of pressure on me.

"Under Ray Rhodes and Mike Sherman, we wanted to stretch the field. I wasn't in that plan so much. They had Corey Bradford running fly routes. They had Donald Driver running go routes. They had Bill Schroeder, all guys who were faster than me. I was the more creative guy, they were the speed guys. I wasn't getting the ball a lot, but I've never been one to make excuses. They pay me, and they expect certain things. I just didn't think the offense suited me. I felt out of place."

He wasn't the least bit out of place in this game, though. Freeman entered the overtime with four catches for 75 yards, not counting the 28 yards he'd cost the Vikings when he drew a pass interference penalty on Cris Dishman that set up a second quarter touchdown. It would have been a good night's work for the six-year veteran if he'd played just four quarters, but he was saving something special for Dishman. And for himself.

Still to come was the most improbable and possibly the most spectacular reception in Packer history. Freeman would catch 477 balls in his nine NFL seasons, but the one that would mark his career forever was the one that bounced off his shoulder pads and settled into his hands while his spine was pressed to the soggy turf.

It was a moment that eyewitnesses from both sides would never forget as an abnormally large contingent of Minnesota fans found their way into Lambeau Field for one of the two regular-season contests reserved for Milwaukee season ticket holders. It was late, it was wet, and it was 250 miles round trip. Hundreds decided not to make the drive. Besides, the Packers were logical underdogs.

Minnesota had lost only once in eight weeks. Green Bay had lost three times in a month. The Vikings had Daunte Culpepper, Randy Moss, Cris Carter and Robert Smith. The Packers weren't the same team they'd been under

Minnesota's Cris Dishman (clockwise from photo #1) seems to be in perfect position to intercept the pass but the ball eludes him as Antonio Freeman tumbles to the ground and makes an improbable catch, gets to his feet and runs it in for a 43-yard touchdown before celebrating with the crowd.

Holmgren. The Vikings were on their way to the post-season. The Packers would be making tee times in January after finishing the season 9-7 and missing the playoffs. If the game had been scheduled for the Metrodome, nobody would have given them a chance.

But it was at Lambeau Field where the weather is usually the Packers' friend. The groundskeeper waited until an hour before kickoff before rolling the tarp off the field, and the grass was in decent condition when the game began. But still the Vikings couldn't get out of their own way. They would gain 407 yards to the Packers' 298, but the five turnovers were crucial, while the home team committed none. Culpepper looked badly confused as he threw two balls to Darren Sharper and one to Mike McKenzie. All three of his interceptions were on passes intended for Moss.

Culpepper did find Moss three times for plays that netted 20 yards or more and led to scores in the first half, but Minnesota's star wideout caught only two more balls for 27 yards after the break. More important, he never did find his way into the end zone, something he'd managed to do at least once in his four previous appearances against the Packers.

Moss wasn't the only one who was feeling out of sorts that night. In addition to the turnovers, the Vikings lost 129 yards on 11 penalties. Still, Gary Anderson was set to kick a game winning 33-yard field goal with 7 seconds to play in regulation, but Berger couldn't corral the snap after asking twice for a new ball. When he tried to pick up the ball and run with it, Allen Rossum jumped on his back and persuaded him to throw it to Tyrone Williams. If Berger had spiked the ball, Minnesota might have had time for another play.

"If I wasn't an idiot, I would have spiked the ball," Berger said in the locker room. "For some reason, it didn't cross my mind." A costly omission, but the Vikings were about to make a worse one in overtime.

The Packers were in trouble on their final drive, facing a third and nine on their own 29-yard line, but they stayed in business with Favre's 22-yard pass to Schroeder. After Ahman Green ran for seven yards and then lost one, the teams lined up on the Minnesota 43 where the Vikings changed their defense and Favre threw to Freeman anyway.

"Dishman made a good play on the ball by adjusting his coverage," Freeman said. "He stayed deeper than my slant. I remember reaching over his back just to make sure he wouldn't intercept the football, and I remember him grabbing the top of his head as if to say, 'Aw man, I had an interception.' Meanwhile I was falling toward the ground, and for some reason I looked up to see what the result of the play was, whether he intercepted it or what. I saw the ball on a downward spiral, and it hit my shoulder. My instinct just told me to stick my hands out and catch it before it hit the ground.

"I stuck my hand out and I was able to catch the football, cradle it, get up and make my way to the end zone. The reason I was able to make it to the end zone was that Dishman had grabbed his head, and he was looking toward the sideline. But the play was still going on. Robert Griffith came over from his safety position, but I think he thought the play was dead because he gave me kind of a half-ass run to make a tackle, as if to say 'What's he doing?'"

Everyone else in the stadium seemed to have the same question. Favre, who never saw the catch, hustled downfield, jumped on his receiver's back and whispered into his ear, "Hey, did you catch it?" It was a good question, but he was asking the wrong man. In the confusion, he'd landed on Donald Driver. When he finally got to Freeman, he posed the question again.

"Brett was the first one down there, and he said, 'What? Did you catch it?'" Freeman said. "I said, 'Yeah, I caught it.' and he was like 'Are you serious?' Then he picked me up and said, 'I love you, man. That was a great play.' Then the rest of the offense and all the other players swarmed the field."

The play was reviewed, and Freeman said that was the most nerve-wracking time of the whole night for him. But he was sure he'd caught the ball, and he wasn't surprised that the play stood.

"When it was all over, the guys carried me off the field," he said. "That had never happened to me before. Never. I've seen some pictures of that, and I actually looked like I was about to cry. It was a real emotional play for me. For those guys to pick me up and carry me off like that… I probably did cry. That play just helped me out so much."

Favre signals "Touchdown."

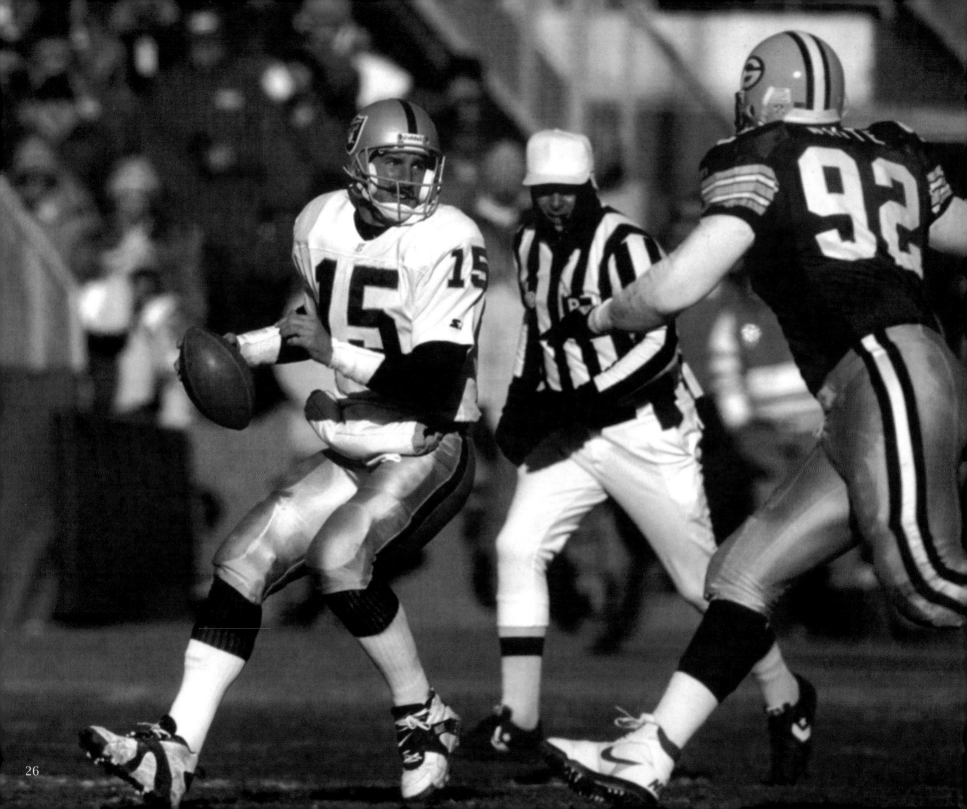

Opposite page: Reggie White closes in on Raiders quarterback Jeff Hostetler, who had a long day, suffering four sacks and an interception. Backup Vince Evans also was sacked four times and threw an interception on the day when the Lambeau Leap was born.

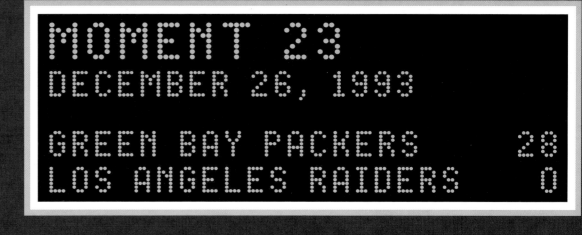

A LEAP OF FAITH

Decisions. Decisions. It was hard enough for the man in the end zone seat to keep his beer from freezing on this zero-degree day, and now he had a human missile soaring at him from the field of play. What was it going to be? Fetch the flying Packer or defend his brew?

He went for the catch as LeRoy Butler raced across the goal line and just kept going until he'd launched himself into the storied stands at Lambeau Field. Forget Joe Horn's cell phone, Terrell Owens' Sharpie or Randy Moss' infamous "moon." The Lambeau Leap was born.

Or christened might be more like it. "Oh my God, I had beer spilled all over me," Butler said as he looked back on his historic flight. "I have no idea who the guy was, but he had to make up his mind whether to catch me or drink that beer. And after I jumped up there, he whispered in my ear, 'You owe me a beer.' I told the guys on the sideline about it, and they just died laughing."

At the time, everyone else seemed to be missing the punch line. The Leap was born without a name or a bit of fanfare. There wasn't a single mention of it in any of the six stories written about the game in the next day's *Milwaukee Journal.* Not one picture or even a speck of small type.

It was almost as if Wisconsin had forgotten how to celebrate a major Green Bay victory, there being so few of them in the past 20 years. Just seeing a Packer in the end zone was surprising enough. No one gave much thought to what he'd do next.

John Jurkovic hitches a ride on Hostetler. Jurkovic had 2 ½ sacks in the game.

"We made a big deal out of it as players, and the fans thought it was cool," said Butler. "But we thought it was just going to die. But once we got connected a year later, it just sort of picked up again. It was amazing that people kept referring to it. I don't even remember who named it. Some media person I think called it the 'Lambeau Leap.'

"Robert Brooks made it famous. Every time he scored he would jump up there, and then other guys would score, and they'd go flying into the stands. People just loved it. It wasn't the 50-yard line seats you wanted anymore, it was the first three or four rows in the end zone. There are no bad seats at Lambeau Field, but the end zone used to be a kind of downgradeable seat. Now it's a reward because you could catch a player there at any minute. We're going to have to change the ticket prices. "

No question the Packers were worth the price of admission that day. After losing to the Vikings in Milwaukee the week before, they needed to win to stay in the race for their first playoff spot in a decade. Two decades if you discount the strike-shortened 1982 season. They were 8-6 with a season-ending date with Detroit coming up the following Sunday. If they could win these last two games, they could wrap up the Central Division championship. They wound up splitting them instead, but they still got into the post-season as a wild card.

It wasn't the most important home game in the team's history, but it was the most significant of the last decade, and it signaled the arrival of the golden era of Mike Holmgren and Ron Wolf. It also happened to be the second-coldest game ever played at Lambeau Field.

Zero degrees and a 9 mph wind added up to a minus-22 wind chill at kickoff, although conditions were improving. The mercury rocketed to 2 degrees at 2 p.m. and all the way to 3 an hour after that before falling again. Quarterback Brett Favre told *The Journal* that he'd rubbed Vaseline "in places where I never thought I'd put it." A Raiders official who'd clearly never been on a Wisconsin deer hunt looked at the stands and asked, "What's all that orange clothing for?"

"It was one of the coldest days of my life," Butler said. "People were wondering why we even had to play in that stuff."

It was 70 degrees in Los Angeles when the Raiders climbed on the plane for Green Bay, taking with them the wrong mind set, the wrong personnel and the wrong shoes. They came expecting to play a football game, and the Iditarod broke out. A team built on speed, they didn't have the traction they needed to go long or the running backs they needed to pound inside. Their cleats became

skate blades, while the Packers ran by them in turf shoes.

The Raiders gained only 46 yards on the ground, and Nick Bell, their frostbitten running back, fumbled twice in the second quarter before coach Art Shell yanked him. Oakland's two quarterbacks completed just 18 of 38 passes for 188 yards between them and got sacked 8 times. The Packers, meanwhile, piled up 148 yards rushing, thanks to the work of Edgar Bennett and Darrell Thompson and an offensive line that not only knew where it was going but had the shoes to get there. Favre was sacked only twice for 9 yards in losses, and he passed for 190 yards.

The Packers took a 14-0 lead on Bennett's one-yard run in the second quarter and Favre's 23-yard pass to Sterling Sharpe in the third. If the Raiders weren't dead, they were in the terminal stages of hypothermia. Three plays into the final period, their final hope perished.

Vince Evans threw a screen pass to Randy Jordan on the right side, and Butler smacked Jordan, creating both a fumble and a debate. Jordan insisted that he never had control of the ball. Shell agreed, claiming it was an incomplete pass, not a fumble. The officials weren't impressed. Neither was Reggie White, who scooped up the ball and ran 10 yards along the sideline before he was grabbed around the waist by Raider guard Steve Wisniewski. Along came Butler.

"The greatest thing about the play was that we got eye contact," said Butler. "I kind of anticipated him pitching the ball to me because when he was in Philly they did that all the time. If they got in trouble they'd pitch it to the defensive back, and he'd run the ball. We never did that at Green Bay."

There's a first time for everything. White tossed the ball back to Butler as he was going down, and the fourth-year safety did the rest.

"(Linebacker) Johnny Holland hollered, 'Run! Run!'" White told *The Journal* after the game. "If it had been 10 years ago, I probably would have run it in for a touchdown."

Instead, he watched as Butler covered the last 25 yards to the end zone and continued his journey until he'd made the acquaintance of the beer drinker and dozens of his closest neighbors.

"It was just spontaneous," Butler said. "I'm running down the sideline thinking, 'This is cool. This is my first touchdown, and I've got to do something great.' I looked, and nobody was around me, and I thought it would be cool to just kind of jump up there and hug the fans.

"So I threw the ball down and I pointed at the people in that section like I was going to jump. I figured if I didn't point, I'd catch them by surprise. But once I pointed, they rushed down and leaned over like they were going to catch me. Maybe they thought I was going to high five them or something. And they all kind of rushed down, and they were yelling and screaming. It was awesome."

And a little dangerous. Butler said the players were concerned at first that they might hurt somebody by jumping into the stands wearing all that equipment. But as long as the people had fair warning, it wasn't a problem.

"There's no surprise, like there might be if you were at a baseball game and somebody hit a foul ball into the stands," Butler said. "People are waiting for you. They'll get upset if you don't jump in there. You celebrate with your fans, not with some chicken dance or something like that. You're not showing up the other team. You're just showing your love for your fans.

"It's caught on in a lot of other places, too. Every time Randy Moss scored in Minnesota, he'd jump in there. It was the same thing in Kansas City. I talked to players on other teams, and they said the fans were writing letters to them asking them if they're going to jump into the stands. But it's always referred to as the Lambeau Leap."

Butler had a lot of big moments in his 12 years with the Packers, but he ranks the Leap as the most memorable because of the impact it had on so many people. It helped, too, that the Packers won that day and then went on to beat Detroit in the wild card game before losing to Dallas in the divisional playoff.

"I just know that that was the start of our whole organization turning around," he said.

And getting off its feet at the same time.

Opposite page: LeRoy Butler soars into the stands behind the south end zone for Green Bay's first Lambeau Leap.

31

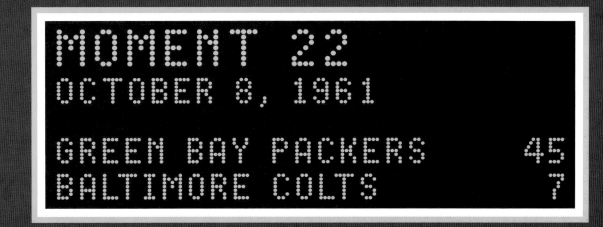

MOMENT 22
OCTOBER 8, 1961

GREEN BAY PACKERS   45
BALTIMORE COLTS   7

CASTING A PAUL ON THE COLTS

A little more than two minutes into the game, Paul Hornung had a touchdown. Forty-three minutes later, he had four touchdowns. And a field goal. And six extra points.

Running, kicking, catching, throwing — it seemed there was nothing Hornung couldn't do to score points on the Baltimore Colts, but that was the easy part. Scoring points with Vince Lombardi was always harder.

The most productive one-man show in Packers history ended with Hornung putting up a team record 33 points, running 11 times for 111 yards, catching three passes for 28 yards and even throwing for a touchdown that was called back on a penalty. Only two people had ever scored more in a single NFL game, but if Lombardi was awed, he didn't let it show.

"It was a great team effort on the part of both groups — the offense and the defense," he said at his post-game press conference. "I don't see how you can single out any one player."

Most coaches might have found a way, but instead of singling out Hornung, Lombardi took him out. Clear out of the game after the third quarter. It was a fine gesture toward Colts coach Weeb Ewbank, but there's no telling how many points it cost Hornung. Lombardi didn't care. "We're not interested in records of any type," he told the reporters.

Hornung, on the other hand, is still kind of interested, or at least curious. "I had a whole quarter to go," he said, looking back on his record-setting afternoon. "There's no telling how many points I could have scored. I had a shot at 50."

By the end of the third quarter he'd already scored 31 to the Colts' 7, but Lombardi had a point. Hornung did get some help from a defense that forced eight turnovers, and from fullback Jim Taylor, who took over the NFL rushing lead that day with an 82-yard game, and from Willie Wood who returned a punt 72 yards for a fourth-quarter touchdown. But there's no question this was Hornung's day.

This performance was hardly off the charts for him, however. He led the league in scoring for the third straight season in 1961 with 146 points, and that wasn't even a career best. The year before, he'd set the NFL record at 176, a mark that lasted until San Diego's LaDainian Tomlinson broke it in 2006. Tomlinson played 16 games that year. Hornung played a 12-game schedule in 1960.

Four years later, he would pick on the Colts again, this time scoring five touchdowns on the road. But he had to settle for 30 points because he was no longer the Packers' place-kicker.

Hornung is a target of another Starr pass.

"It seemed like I always had good runs against Baltimore," Hornung recalled. "The day I had the five touchdowns we needed to win to get in the playoffs. I always kidded Gale Sayers because that was the day he had six touchdowns against the 49ers in Chicago. I told him, 'Your game didn't mean anything. Ours was for the championship of the Western Division.'"

There would be five Western championships in the nine seasons Hornung played for the Packers, but those didn't start until Lombardi got to Green Bay. In 1957 Lisle Blackbourn drafted Hornung out of Notre Dame in the first round as a quarterback, and he didn't seem to know what to do with him. Neither did Scooter McLean the following season. Some days Hornung was a quarterback, some days he was a fullback and some days a halfback.

When Lombardi arrived in 1959, Hornung became a fixture at halfback, a development Baltimore in particular would have cause to regret. The Colts were a fierce rival for the Packers in those days, and no one was expecting a rout when they came to town on a balmy October Sunday.

But the visitors had barely finished their pre-game stretches when Hornung was off on a 54-yard touchdown run that he followed with the extra point.

"Paul was not the greatest speedster in the world," said tight end Gary Knafelc. "Actually, he was probably one of the slowest guys we had, but when coach Lombardi had us go up and diagram plays, Paul knew where his blocking was coming from all the time. No one cut off his blockers better than he did, and no one set up blockers better.

"If you look at Paul's great runs, they were not on the sidelines outrunning anybody. They were coming back against the grain and running with blockers. On that 54-yard run, there was nobody around him. Everybody had been knocked down."

The Colts recovered from that shock by tying the game with a 72-yard drive, but Hornung was just getting his legs under him. His 38-yard field goal put the Packers ahead for good, and then he scored from the one, which was more familiar territory for him.

"Of all the running backs I've seen over the years both as a player and as a coach, I think Hornung was the best inside the 5 or inside the 10," said Lew Carpenter, who played for 10 years and coached for more than 30 during his NFL days. "He just had a knack for smelling the goal line."

While Hornung was sniffing out the end zone, the Packers' defense was smelling blood. Johnny Unitas completed only 11 of 24 passes, and he had five intercepted, while another pick was nullified by a penalty. Unitas also lost a fumble, and Lamar McHan, who replaced Unitas in the fourth quarter, threw another interception.

A sellout crowd of 38,669 thoroughly enjoyed the defensive dominance, but it was Hornung who continued to steal the show in the third quarter by adding an eight-yard touchdown pass from Bart Starr and a 10-yard scoring run following an interception by Wood. Even after he took a seat in the fourth quarter, Hornung came back to kick a couple of extra points just to remind Baltimore that he was still around. As if the Colts could ever forget.

"It seemed that the defense was made for me with a lot of teams, and Taylor would have a tougher time," Hornung said. "We played in a two-back system, and Taylor was always scoring 15 or 20 touchdowns, and I was, too."

Which would help explain how he finished his career with 760 points, second to the legendary Don Hutson when he retired and still fourth-best in the Packers' history. Of course there were other explanations.

"Put Paul inside the 5-yard-line, and I'd rather have him than anybody," Max McGee said. "He was a great athlete and a great scorer."

Lombardi couldn't have said it better himself. Not that he would.

Paul Hornung receives the NFL's MVP award while Chicago's Mike Ditka gets the Rookie of the Year trophy from sportscaster Chris Schenkel following the 1961 season. Hornung scored a club record 33 points against the Baltimore Colts in the fourth game of the year and led the NFL in scoring with 146.

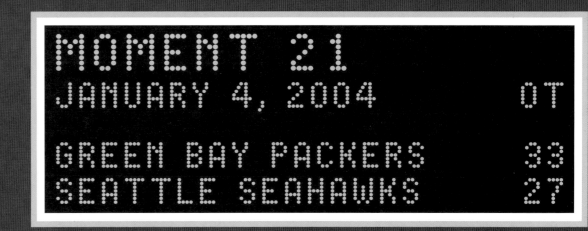

```
MOMENT 21
JANUARY 4, 2004                    OT

GREEN BAY PACKERS                  33
SEATTLE SEAHAWKS                   27
```

DAYS OF DESTINY

There had been so much talk of "destiny" you half expected a hand to drop out of the sky and give Al Harris a high five as he waved his left arm in the air on the way to the end zone.

The 71,457 faithful who were on their feet at Lambeau Field on this brilliant Sunday had reason to believe that Harris' dramatic 52-yard interception in the Packers' wild card victory over Mike Holmgren's Seattle Seahawks was just the first step on a return route to the Super Bowl. But a stunning disappointment in the NFC divisional playoff game in Philadelphia would prove that "destiny" makes a lame substitute for a good prevent defense. If the fans had known that fourth-and-26 was in their future, they might have left those "We Believe" signs home.

But that was a week away, and wide receiver Donald Driver wasn't getting much argument when he declared that the Packers had angels watching over them. Just making the playoffs had required a small miracle. This team had gone into the bye week with a 3-4 record, and it was still only 6-6 with four games to go after getting spanked, 22-14, at Detroit. Even beating Chicago, San Diego, Oakland and Denver in those four games wouldn't have been enough if Minnesota's collapsible Vikings hadn't found a way to lose their final game.

A last second touchdown catch by Nathan Poole had given the Arizona Cardinals a come-from-behind victory at the Metrodome the week before, putting the Packers in the post-season and Poole in the stands in Green Bay. He was there as the guest of Mayor Jim Schmitt, although the Packers organization didn't invite him to their locker room or anywhere else out of respect to the Vikings.

Packer loyalists had taken it as further evidence that somebody up there liked them when Brett Favre turned in the game of his life in Oakland on December 22, the day after his father died of a heart attack. This was the same Favre who was playing championship quality quarterback with his right thumb in a splint, having broken it 11 weeks earlier. Who does that without divine intervention?

Former Packer Matt Hasselbeck launches one of his 45 passes. He completed 25 for 305 yards, but lived to regret his coin toss boast and his final throw.

Fate also sent the kind of weather calculated to help the home team. The temperature at kickoff was 20 degrees, and a swirling gale blew debris all over the stadium and put the wind chill factor at 7 degrees. Favre had played 36 games at home with the temperature at 34 or below, and Green Bay had won 35 of them.

Even the choice of opponent seemed to be ideal. The Packers had routed the Seahawks, 35-13, at Lambeau Field in October, and they had plenty of extra motivation to make it a series sweep. Who would they rather send home unhappy than Holmgren, the man who had taken eight assistant coaches and most of the front office with him when he'd left the organization five years earlier?

"Everybody really wanted to beat the old ball coach," Harris recalled. "We knew we were good enough to advance, and it wasn't so much destiny with us as the whole thing about Mike Holmgren coming back. We were just going to go out and try to play hard and win the game."

The Seahawks were led by quarterback Matt Hasselbeck, who was hoping to make a triumphant return after serving as Favre's understudy for two years. Hasselbeck was surplus goods when the Packers traded him and the 17th choice in the 2001 draft to Seattle for the 10th pick and a third-round choice, but the deal couldn't have worked out much worse. Green Bay squandered the 10th pick on the vanishing Jamal Reynolds and wasted the third rounder on the disappointing Torrance Marshall, while the Seahawks landed future all-pro guard Steve Hutchinson at 17.

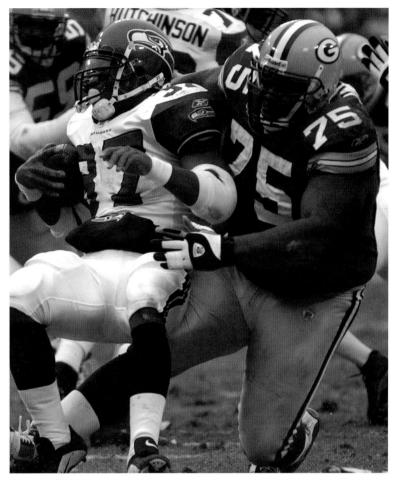

Grady Jackson stacks up Seattle running back Shaun Alexander, who was held to 45 yards on 20 carries.

But the Packers had already gotten some redemption for the Hasselbeck deal by heisting running back Ahman Green from Holmgren for a forgettable cornerback named Fred Vinson. In 2003, Green had rushed for 1,883 yards, while Favre had led the league in touchdown passes, and the defense had produced 32 takeaways. All things considered, this may have been the only real Super Bowl-caliber team the Packers had had since Holmgren left.

But the Seahawks gave them all they could eat that Sunday, and they could easily have been the ones going on to Philadelphia if Harris hadn't literally stepped in and stolen the game. With 4:16 gone in overtime and the Seahawks facing a third and 11 on their 45, Hasselbeck could see the Packers were coming with a mortgage-the-ranch blitz, and he audibled to a three-step drop, sending wide receiver Alex Bannister on a hitch route. That's when Harris decided it was time to take a chance.

As Bannister stopped 9 yards down the field and looked back for the ball, Harris stepped in front of him, picked off the pass and sprinted 52 yards to the end zone, most of it with his left hand in the air.

"We actually practiced against that play," Harris said. "All of the West Coast teams have it in their arsenal against an all-out blitz. Everybody knows I play bump and run, and (assistant defensive backfield coach) Lionel Washington would say, 'Al, I want you to let the rush get there, and maybe you can steal a pick.'

"Hasselbeck had checked to that call two plays earlier, and the guy did the same thing. He ran a stop, and when I saw that, I thought, 'No, he can't be about to do the same play.' If I had broken a little earlier, I probably would have overrun the ball. I really didn't believe he'd make that same check, but he did."

The danger, Harris said, was that Hasselbeck would pump fake and Bannister would turn the play upfield. If he had, it probably would have been a touchdown because there was nobody behind Harris. But veteran cornerbacks live for opportunities like that. "It's a matter of trusting your system and hoping the rush gets there," he said. "The next year, we had that exact same defense against Minnesota, and they called the same route, and Randy Moss took it upfield and did that mooning thing after he scored. The thing is, one guy didn't blitz that time, and so the quarterback had time to adjust. Randy made a one-handed catch, and they won the game. So I wouldn't say it's so much a gamble as just trusting that everybody is going to do their job."

Hasselbeck certainly did his, except for that final pick. He led the Seahawks on drives of 74, 77 and 67 yards in the second half as Seattle tied the game with 51 seconds left in regulation on Shaun Alexander's third one-yard touchdown run of the day. At that point, the Seahawks looked unstoppable, which was at least part of the reason why Hasselbeck got a little carried away when the captains gathered at midfield for the overtime coin flip.

Seattle won the flip, and the young quarterback was only half right when he proclaimed loudly and boldly, "We want the ball. We're going to score."

Those might have been fighting words if the Packers' defense had been paying any attention. "I never heard him say it," Harris said. "I only heard about it after the game, and then I was like 'He said what?'"

Harris' deeds proved to be more effective than Hasselbeck's words as the last pass of the game ended up in the cornerback's hands. The Packers were on their way to Philadelphia, but "destiny" declined to go along for the ride.

Opposite page: Harris gets the game ball from Mike Sherman in the Green Bay locker room.

Opposite page: David Whitehurst directs the Green Bay offense against New England in the Packers first Monday night game at Lambeau Field. With Lynn Dickey still struggling to come back from a 1977 injury, Whitehurst started at quarterback and completed 17 of 27 passes for 206 yards and scored the clinching touchdown on a four-yard run.

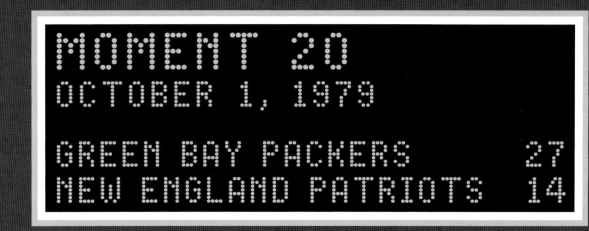

MOMENT 20
OCTOBER 1, 1979

GREEN BAY PACKERS   27
NEW ENGLAND PATRIOTS   14

MONDAY FUNNIES

Monday *Night Football* was coming to Lambeau Field for the first time ever, but it wasn't the Packers who the viewers were tuning in to watch.

Mediocre talent and bad lighting had limited the franchise to three home appearances in ABC's first nine years of prime time football, and all three of those were in Milwaukee. Now only the lighting had improved as the Packers entered the 1,000th game in their history.

On one side of the field were the defending AFC East champion New England Patriots with a 3-1 record and seven first-round draft choices in their lineup, including future Hall of Fame players John Hannah and Mike Haynes. The other five all played in at least one Pro Bowl.

On the other side of the field were the 1-3 Packers, injury ridden, distracted and on the decline. After starting the 1978 season 6-1, they had won only two of their last nine games, and they weren't looking any better in '79. They had suffered three losses to division opponents, and the most recent one had coach Bart Starr answering some pointed questions.

Naturally, ABC's Don Meredith, Howard Cosell and Frank Gifford were giving the home team little chance, but they had it all wrong, and so did just about everyone else. The Packers had a big surprise in store for the Patriots, for the television audience and, most of all, for themselves.

"I remember watching all the film that week," recalled quarterback Lynn Dickey, who was still recovering from a broken leg suffered in the ninth game of the '77 season and playing behind David Whitehurst. "I kept thinking, 'I don't see any weakness on this team.' Offensively, they were really good, and defensively I thought they were even better. I remember telling my brother, 'I don't see any way in hell we can win this game.'"

It was a logical conclusion, especially in light of what had happened the week before. The Packers had had the ball and the wind at their backs on their 25-yard line with 1:41 to play in regulation at Minnesota, and Starr had elected to go with three runs and play for overtime. Minnesota responded by scoring on the first possession of the extra period and winning the game. Afterwards, frustrated receiver James Lofton slammed his helmet and shoulder pads into his locker while the team was kneeling in prayer, an ironic reaction to a coach who'd asked for patience and prayers.

Looking back at Starr's strategy at Minnesota, Whitehurst said, "He probably did it to protect me. He probably didn't have confidence in me to lead them down the field without making a mistake."

Starr denied any lack of faith in the offense at his Monday press conference following the game, but he did admit that he wouldn't have stayed employed with a five-year record of 22-39-1 if he'd been anyone else. Nevertheless, his job seemed safe. His contract had three years to run, and he still had the confidence of Packers President Dominic Olejniczak. The trick was to make sure his players felt the same way about him. The Patriots game was a long step in that direction.

"I remember watching New England on tape, and this was probably the only

Terdell Middleton (34) and Barty Smith (33), opposite page, started in the Packers' backfield and combined for 119 yards rushing and two touchdowns.

time in my whole career that I thought, 'We don't have a chance against these guys,'" said center Larry McCarren. "I probably should have thought it more.

"Bart was into power point presentations on an overhead and stuff like that before they were in vogue, which was a fine thing. But at the morning meeting before the game, instead of doing something like that, which he normally would have done, he told us about the only time he had been in a street fight. He was comparing the game to a street fight, and he really spoke from the heart. It was a real good way to set the stage for the game, and I thought it had an impact."

Mike Douglass thought so, too. The linebacker recalled that most of the players were nervous in the week leading up to the game. They didn't want to look bad in their first appearance at home on *Monday Night Football*, and they didn't want to appear overmatched by the talented Patriots.

Douglass said they knew this was one of the biggest games they would play and they would have to step things up a level. He believes Starr did just that with his pre-game speech.

"It just sounded more firm than the soft Bart we were used to," Douglass said. "He actually sounded like a head coach who wanted to win a really big game."

The coach may also have had some extra incentive. Two years earlier, New England had smoked Green Bay, 38-3, in a pre-season game at Milwaukee County Stadium, and Starr had accused coach Chuck Fairbanks of running up the score.

But he denied that revenge was a factor, pointing out that New England had a different coach and different players. And then he set about making sure that everything about this game was different as well.

Gone was Green Bay's normal conservative offense. The Packers tried a double pass, a reverse from their own 30-yard line and a fake field goal. They passed 14 times on first down, including once from their own end zone, and they gambled by going for a first down on fourth-and-one at the New England 47 late in the third quarter.

The gamble didn't work. A lot of things didn't work, but enough did to keep the Patriots' defense guessing all night. Whitehurst threw a couple of interceptions, but he also gained 206 yards by completing 17 of 27 passes, including one that went 15 yards to Aundra Thompson for a touchdown

"Whitehurst didn't have the best talent in the world," said tackle Greg Koch, "but he had a lot of intangibles. Players wanted to win for him. If he threw an interception, he was down there trying to make a tackle. He was throwing blocks on running plays. He was just a tough, blue-collar guy."

And he was accompanied that night by a tough, blue-collar defense with a few surprises of its own for Patriots quarterback Steve Grogan. The Packers started the game in a 3-4 alignment instead of their normal 4-3, and they used it frequently on passing downs. They shifted personnel around throughout the game, and they blitzed much more than usual. The result was five sacks, five interceptions, a fumble recovery and a bewildered Grogan.

"They let us open up a little more," Douglass said. "I think a reality check was put in place to say, 'Hey, we do have enough talent to actually play, so give us a chance to do something and not just sit there like ducks so people could pick us off.'

"We tried to put pressure on Grogan. We didn't think he was that mobile. We just went after him. We tried to make him get rid of the ball."

On one of the first times Grogan got rid of it, he threw a 27-yard touchdown pass to tight end Russ Francis, staking the Patriots to a 7-0 lead halfway through the first quarter. But then a sellout crowd that had begun filling the parking lots 4½ hours before game time in a drizzle watched contentedly as the Packers scored the next 20 points.

Johnnie Gray's interception set up a one-yard touchdown run by Barty Smith late in the first period, and then Whitehurst finished a 74-yard drive with his touchdown pass to Thompson. Terdell Middleton's 1-yard run made it 20-7 after Steve Luke intercepted Grogan on the New England 20 midway through the second quarter. But Chester Marcol had the extra point blocked, and the Pats were able to close the difference to 20-14 at halftime when Grogan finished an 83-yard drive with a 6-yard pass to Francis.

At that point, the Patriots had out-gained Green Bay 258 yards to 167, but they got only 143 yards the rest of the way, and the Packers didn't even need their final touchdown. It came anyway, on Whitehurst's 4-yard run, and once again an interception set the stage. This one was by cornerback Mike McCoy on the fifth play of the third period.

All four of the Packers' defensive backs intercepted passes that night, and all 45 players got game balls, something that hadn't happened since Starr's first victory as a coach in 1975 at Dallas. This game might have been as big as that one for Starr. "It was a big deal," said Whitehurst. "I was probably too naïve to understand the importance of it all."

It certainly wasn't lost on Starr, although the team would lose four of its next five games on the way to a 5-11 season. But for at least one night, with people watching from coast to coast, the Packers looked as good as anyone in the NFL.

David Whitehurst had his teammates' respect.

Mike Douglass saw a different Starr.

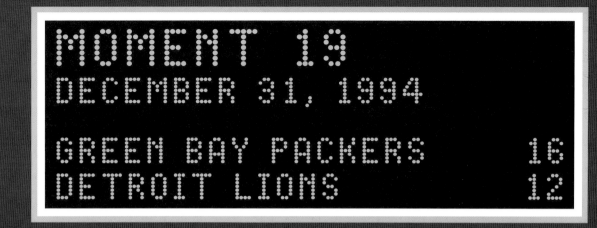

*Opposite page: Barry Sanders
has nowhere to go on a day
when he was held to minus-one
yard rushing on 13 attempts in
the Packers first home playoff
game in 12 years.*

MOMENT 19
DECEMBER 31, 1994

GREEN BAY PACKERS   16
DETROIT LIONS   12

BARRY-ED

They had the best back on the planet in their huddle and 5 minutes and 27 seconds to cover 49 yards on their final drive, and the Detroit Lions gave Barry Sanders the ball exactly twice. It was one way of saying, "What's the use?"

Sanders picked up a yard on the first carry and two on the second, which was practically a gold rush for him on this day when Fritz Shurmur's one-track mind sent the Packers to the second round of the playoffs. It was the worst game of a Hall of Fame career for Sanders, who netted minus-one yard on 13 carries as Green Bay's defensive coordinator dared the Lions to find someone else to beat his team.

They almost did, too. On the 12th play of Detroit's last drive, Dave Krieg threw a 17-yard pass to Herman Moore, but Moore caught the ball in the air and landed with both feet outside the end zone, clinching a victory for the Packers in their first post-season home game in 12 years.

The two teams had met twice before that year, with two decidedly different outcomes. The Packers won, 38-30, in Milwaukee in November, but then Sanders ran over them for 188 yards in a 34-31 Detroit victory a month later. Shurmur was determined not to let that happen again as he prepared for the rubber match.

"Everybody came into the meeting room on Monday, and Fritz said, 'We've got Barry Sanders next week, and I've got a game plan that will blow your socks off,'" recalled safety LeRoy Butler. "We're thinking, 'What's he talking about?' What he meant was, 'Take your shot at Barry. Don't wait. Just go at him. And if you go at him, we've got another guy flying in

49

Frank Winters congratulates Dorsey Levens after his three-yard touchdown run.

there, and another guy flying in there, and eventually we'll get him.' That was our whole goal.

"We had 11 people going to the ball and trying to corral him. We were just going to play cat and mouse with the pass. It was like those World War I fighter planes where you lock onto a target, push 'Fire!' and you can't pull back."

It helped that the local squadron was taking off from frozen grass. Sanders was merely terrific on natural surfaces, whereas he was virtually unstoppable on turf, and the conditions on this day hardly suited his style. It was a cloudy 33 degrees at kickoff, and both the temperature and the players continued to fall throughout the first half. Sanders, who had averaged 5.7 yards a carry while gaining a league-high 1,883 yards during the regular season, carried seven times before the break and lost a net 6 yards in the process.

In his autobiography *Green and Golden Moments*, Packers President Bob Harlan said that general manager Ron Wolf was so pleased with those numbers that he suggested at halftime that the team turn the heater off under the field to keep it slick. Harlan wasn't sure whether Wolf was serious or not, but he politely declined. Not that Shurmur's group needed any help from the grounds crew.

Sanders would be caught behind the line of scrimmage six times in his 13 carries, with half of those stops being made by linebacker Bryce Paup. Meanwhile, Krieg, a Wisconsin native, completed 17 passes for 199 yards, and the Packers could definitely live with that.

"The weather was cold, and we were hoping the field would play to our advantage," said nose tackle John Jurkovic. "We thought Barry Sanders was more dangerous than their quarterback was going to be. Sanders had embarrassed us a ton, but guess what? When you play Barry Sanders, you're going to get embarrassed sometimes. Fritz came in and said, 'This is the way we're going to stop him.' Then once you start stopping him early in the game you kind of build on the momentum. You go, 'Oh my God, we're finding a way to get it done.'

"The other key thing was moving Reggie White inside. Reggie didn't rush from the defensive end that game, he rushed right up the middle over Shawn Bouwens. Bouwens was a young kid from Nebraska Wesleyan, and he couldn't handle Reggie at all. Fritz moved Reggie in there, so you couldn't run away from him. What Fritz wanted to do was move the line of scrimmage with penetration three yards up-field and take away Sanders' cutbacks. Butler moved up in the box, too. When they were going to run the ball, we were like, 'Fine. We're here. We're going to have a party.'"

The party started after the Packers moved 76 yards in 14 plays to take a 7-0 lead on their first possession. Mel Gray returned the kickoff 30 yards to give the Lions good field position on their own 38, but when Sanders got the ball on their first play from scrimmage, cornerback Doug Evans and linebacker George Koonce dumped him for a 2-yard loss. He did gain 7 yards on second down, but that was the last good news he got all day. Sanders lost 6 yards on the next play, and Detroit punted for the first of eight times. The pattern was set.

The Packers' only problem was that they were stopping both teams. Even though they out-gained the Lions, 336 yards to 171 and doubled their 9 first downs, they never led by more than 10 points. Chris Jacke's 51-yard field goal put them up, 10-0, at halftime, but Jacke also missed a 37-yard attempt early in the second quarter. A third-quarter drive died at the Lions' 38 when Edgar Bennett was stopped for no gain on two straight plays, and a combination of dropped passes and over-throws limited the Packers' offense to two more Jacke

Reggie White and Sean Jones were big factors in Sanders' frustrating afternoon. Defensive coordinator Fritz Shurmur moved White to defensive tackle to exploit a weakness on Detroit's offensive line.

field goals.

Quarterback Brett Favre had a respectable day with 23 completions in 38 attempts, playing with a major tummy ache and without all-pro receiver Sterling Sharpe. Favre had missed practice that week with abdominal pains related to the car accident he'd had in college. Sharpe was out with what turned out to be a career-ending neck injury, leaving Robert Brooks to pick up the slack with 7 catches for 88 yards.

The Lions were able to cut their deficit to 10-3 on Jason Hanson's 38-yard field goal in the third quarter, and they made it 13-10 early in the fourth when Gray's 68-yard kickoff return set up a 3-yard touchdown pass from Krieg to Brett Perriman. Jacke's 28-yard field goal wrapped up the Packers' scoring with 5:35 to play and left the Lions to go on their futile final march.

Eric Lynch returned the kickoff 27 yards to get them started in Green Bay territory at the 49, and eight plays later they had a first down on the 13. But then Krieg threw incomplete and Sanders was held to 2 yards. At the 2-minute warning, Detroit was down to its last two plays. Paup came up with a 6-yard sack on the first one, and Moore caught Krieg's pass over the end line on the second. Fittingly, the end zone he stepped out of was the same one that Bart Starr had stepped into to win the Ice Bowl game 27 years earlier to the day.

This victory was hardly as momentous as that one, but it did come with its own hyperbole. "Wasn't that a fabulous game?" said Wolf. "Sanders didn't even gain a yard. To take a player of that caliber and completely shut him down is like going against Sandy Koufax and hitting three or four grand slams. Unbelievable."

And statistically significant. The Lions set a playoff record by winding up with a negative-four yards on 15 rushes, which even surprised the Packers.

"That was amazing what the defense did that day, holding probably one of the top three running backs of all time," said center Frank Winters. "We knew the defense was playing well, but we didn't know until the game was over that Sanders had negative rushing yards. You don't talk about it during the game. It's not like in baseball where the pitcher is throwing a no-hitter, and he knows it the whole game. But after the game is over, you're amazed."

LeRoy Butler (36) and Terrell Buckley (27) close in on Lions receiver Aubrey Matthews

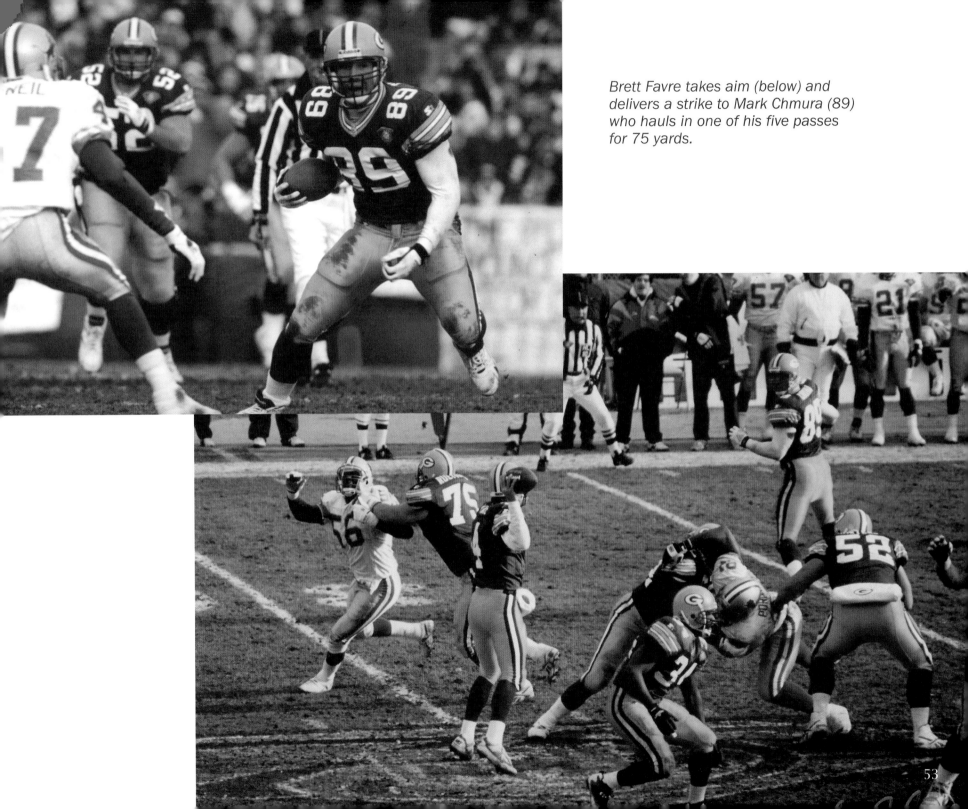

Brett Favre takes aim (below) and delivers a strike to Mark Chmura (89) who hauls in one of his five passes for 75 yards.

53

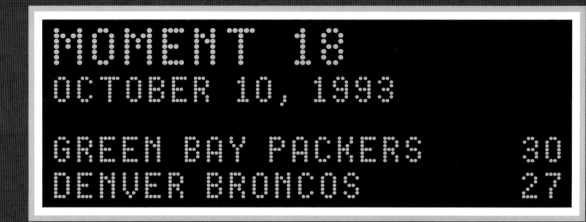

MOMENT 18
OCTOBER 10, 1993

GREEN BAY PACKERS   30
DENVER BRONCOS   27

RUSH TO JUDGMENT

Just in case the Denver Broncos forgot who they were dealing with, the crowd was happy to supply the name.
"Reggie! Reggie! Reggie!" they chanted, a sound Lambeau Field would hear a lot over the next six years. But this was the beginning of it all.

Two plays. One right after the other. The irresistible force encountering the highly movable object. Reggie White vs. John Elway with a nationally-televised Sunday night game and maybe a season on the line. When Elway hit the ground both times, all doubt vanished. Yes indeed, Reggie White was worth the money.

Ron Wolf had shocked the league by signing the perennial all-pro to a four-year, $17 million contract during the off-season, and now everyone knew why.

This wasn't how the NFL's new free agency system was expected to work. Superstars like White weren't supposed to land in little backwaters like Green Bay. Not even the Packer players could believe that would happen.

"I remember walking by the training room and seeing this big guy sitting there in shorts," said safety LeRoy Butler. "I'm like, 'That's Reggie White.' I was like a little kid. I almost went over there and asked for his autograph, and then it dawned on me that I'd been playing for a couple of years.

"I had just seen on TV that he was going to go to San Francisco for a four-year deal or whatever. I had no idea he had signed with us and was doing his physical. I thought he was just going to make a visit. Getting him was great."

Using him was better, although not immediately. White had 1½ sacks in his first four games for Green Bay, which was

Elway goes down on consecutive plays in the final two minutes of the fourth quarter.

respectable but not very satisfying when the Packers lost three of them. After hammering the Los Angeles Rams in their opener, they'd dropped three in a row to Philadelphia, Minnesota and Dallas, and the players were concerned enough to hold a team meeting before the 3-1 Broncos came to town.

"It was getting brutal," said nose tackle John Jurkovic. "I remember thinking after we lost the Philadelphia game on a late touchdown that that was one we should have won. And I think Reggie really started second guessing. It was 'Oh boy, what did I do here?'

"Then we had two road games against the Vikings and Dallas. We got crunched in Dallas, so we came back and started reassessing. I think that's when the lads put things together and said, 'All right. Let's find a way to figure this out.'"

They appeared to have come to the right conclusions when the Packers raced to a 17-0 lead on Denver before the game was 15 minutes old. Chris Jacke kicked a 28-yard field goal, and John Stephens and Edgar Bennett scored on 1-yard runs before Elway put the Broncos on the board with a 14-yard touchdown pass to Vance Johnson. The Packers weren't fazed. Brett Favre connected with Jackie Harris for 66 yards and a touchdown, and Jacke added a pair of second-quarter field goals to make it a 30-7 game at halftime.

The viewers had every reason to think they were witnessing a rout, but the quarterbacks had a surprise in store for them. Both quarterbacks.

After completing 13 of 20 passes for 182 yards in the first half, Favre, who turned 24 that day, inexplicably began acting his age. He went 7 for 12 the rest of the way, including three balls he threw to the Broncos.

"You know he had that great second year — his first in Green Bay — and he kind of slid after that," said tight end Mark Chmura. "Those were the years when Mike Holmgren would just tear into him, because he could. Those were some tough times for him. Brett wasn't the superstar he became in '95 and '96."

Elway, on the other hand, was definitely Elway. He had already led the Broncos on 31 game-saving fourth quarter drives in his career, and the 32nd seemed imminent. He began by moving Denver from its own 16-yard line to the Packers' 36 on the first series of the third quarter, but White put a stop to that when he sacked Elway on a fourth-and-16 play. But then the Broncos scored the game's next 20 points.

Linebacker Mike Croel returned Favre's first interception 22 yards for a touchdown, and then Elway took Denver on a 68-yard touchdown drive on its next possession with Rod Bernstine running it in from the 2. Jason Elam closed the difference to 30-27 with a pair of field goals, the second coming after another Favre interception. With 8:31 to play, the Broncos had wiped out all but three points of a 23-point deficit, and they were feeling pretty good about themselves.

"We made a lot of mistakes in the secondary," Butler said. "It was so easy at the beginning of the game, but you know good teams are going to make a run. When they started coming back, they got real arrogant. They were shaking their heads and saying, 'We told you we were coming back.'

"Then you started thinking about what Elway had

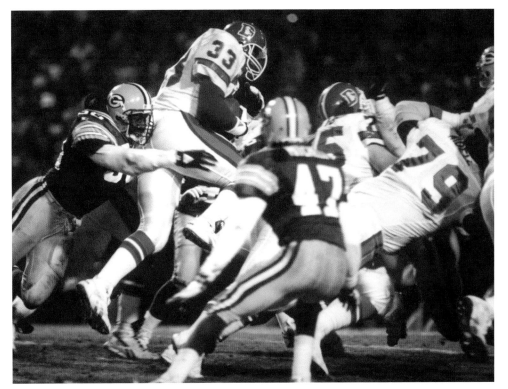
The Packers' defense engulfs Denver running back Rod Bernstine.

done in the past with all those comebacks, and you had to figure you were at a disadvantage. It was like giving somebody new life. You poke an animal with a stick, and it will come after you if you open the cage. That's what we did. We gave them too many opportunities."

And then Favre gave them one more.

After an exchange of punts following Elam's second field goal, Favre was facing a third and 3 on his own 24 yard line when Denver blitzed safeties Steve Atwater and Dennis Smith. Smith hit Favre just as he was throwing a pass for Harris, and when the ball came up short, Denver nickel back Le-Lo Lang was there to pick it off. With 2:05 to play, the Broncos had possession at the Green Bay 43 and the league's most dangerous quarterback in charge.

"They had us on the ropes," Butler acknowledged. "But then Reggie stepped up. It's almost unfair to have somebody like Reggie on your side because he could pick his spots like Muhammad Ali with the 'rope-a-dope.' When the fourth quarter came around, it was like he said, 'I'm going to take over. Nobody's going to block me. Why even try?'"

It might have been a good question for Russell Freeman, who was lined up against White. Denver's right tackle was a second-year pro who had made the team as a rookie free agent. He started every game at left tackle his first year, and then he'd moved to the right side in 1993. Two years later, he was out of the NFL. That wasn't entirely White's fault, but he did nothing to advance Freeman's career that night.

After a running play and a pass netted nothing for the Broncos, Elway found himself still on the Green Bay 43 with 1:56 on the clock, needing at least 10 yards to get Elam in range for a game-winning field goal. He didn't get an inch.

With Elway in shotgun formation, Packers defensive coordinator Ray Rhodes faked a blitz and rushed three linemen. White raced past Freeman and decked Elway 8 yards behind the line of scrimmage. Now it was fourth and 18 at the Denver 49.

Once again, Elway set up in the shotgun. This time Rhodes went with a four-man rush, and White simply tossed Freeman out of his way. Elway tried to scramble, but White chased him down at the Broncos' 35. With 1:27 to play, the game was over.

"Reggie just went through Freeman," Jurkovic said. "Just went by him. It was a must-pass situation, and Reggie just teed it back and went after Elway. Then the crowd started screaming, 'Reggie! Reggie! Reggie!' It was over after that.

"It was never easy getting to Elway, but Reggie had that hump move, and if you weren't used to it, he'd bring it. He'd get you. But you know what? That's why Reggie got all the money he got paid. In crunch time, that's what he's supposed to do. That's why he's one of the top sackers in NFL history."

That's the way Wolf looked at it, too. The Packers' general manager admitted that he became a "raving maniac" watching the Broncos come back, and as he saw the halftime lead melt away, he expected the visitors to win the game. Until White took over.

"When Reggie decided he was going to play, nobody could block him," Wolf said. "The problem was to get him to do that all the time. He was a fabulous player. I had occasion to see darn near every game Elway played in college. He always had a great ability to get away. But that's what I'm talking about with Reggie White. When Reggie White decided enough was enough, I don't think anybody could top him."

While White was playing, no one did. He retired after the 2000 season with 198 sacks, making him the NFL's all-time leader before Bruce Smith broke his record. He had 13 sacks for the Packers in '93, helping them go from 23rd in the league in defense the previous year to second. Which was as good a reason as any for why they finished 9-7 that year and made the playoffs for the first time since 1982.

The Broncos also made the playoffs in '93, but they only split their last 12 games. Maybe Elway was a little worn out after throwing a career-high 59 passes that night. He completed 33 of them for 367 yards, but he was sacked four times. Nobody had ever thrown more passes against the Packers in a single game.

White also tied a personal record with the Packers that night as they won their 500th game in their 75th season. It was one of nine three-sack games for him at Green Bay, including Super Bowl XXXI.

"I remember standing next to (tackle) Tootie Robbins after Reggie's second sack closed it out," said Chmura. "Tootie volunteered to give up the million he was making to Reggie. I kind of laughed and said I was going to hold him to it. We were so elated. We realized how dominant Reggie was going to be for our team and the fact that we were heading in the right direction."

Robbins kept his money. And Reggie White definitely earned his.

Tight end Jackie Harris takes off after catching one of his five passes for 128 yards. Included was a 66-yard touchdown.

Opposite page: The slop dominated the action when the
Packers won their divisional
playoff with San Francisco en
route to Super Bowl XXXI.

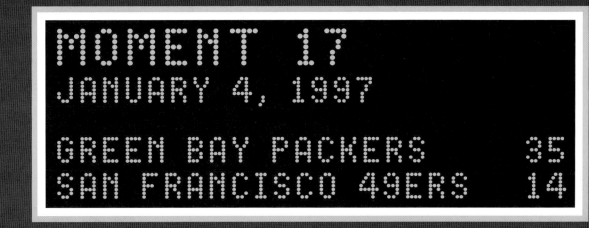

MOMENT 17
JANUARY 4, 1997

GREEN BAY PACKERS   35
SAN FRANCISCO 49ERS   14

SOMETHING SPECIAL

The second half of the crucial divisional playoff game with San Francisco was starting, and Desmond Howard was bringing new meaning to the term "elusive." It seemed neither team could get hold of him.

Green Bay's star kick returner had already scored a touchdown with a 71-yard punt return and set up another one with a 46-yard effort, but where was he now? As Don Beebe prepared for the second-half kickoff, he noticed that he was a single safety. Howard, who was supposed to be standing with him, was nowhere around.

Andre Rison noticed Howard's absence, too, and raced onto the field to take his spot. But he was too late. The 49ers' Jeff Wilkins kicked the ball short and to the left where Howard was supposed to be. It scooted in the mud before Beebe bobbled it, and Steve Israel recovered for San Francisco on the Green Bay 4. Quarterback Elvis Grbac scored on a bootleg on the next snap, and what had once been a 21-0 Packer lead dwindled to 21-14. By then, Howard had found his way to the field.

The vanishing former Heisman Trophy winner had gotten back late after changing his uniform at halftime, which seemed weirdly appropriate on a day so dominated by special teams and weather. Howard's two long returns combined with the punting of Craig Hentrich and a fumbled punt return that set up Green Bay's last scoring drive gave the Packers an enormous advantage. Then again, San Francisco's only scores came as a result of Howard's gaffe and a mistake by Green Bay's punt return team.

None of it came as a huge surprise, given the conditions. A sellout crowd of 60,787, featuring an amazing three no-shows, shivered through a 34-degree, all-day rain that turned the field into a bog. The playing surface was so damaged that day that the league had to re-sod Lambeau Field before the Packers faced Carolina the following week in the NFC

Desmond Howard has clear sailing as he returns a 49ers' kick. Howard returned two punts for 117 yards, including a 71-yarder for the game's first touchdown.

championship game.

The 49ers lost two fumbles in the game, gave up three interceptions and dropped five passes in the first half alone. Three of the drops were committed by a promising rookie wideout named Terrell Owens, who didn't catch a pass all day. The Packers fumbled five times but recovered four of them and had no interceptions.

"It was pure slop," recalled defensive tackle Santana Dotson. "At times, it was raining sideways. But that's why you play the game. It was fun. It reminded you of a pick-up game when you go out and play in the rain."

No wonder Howard wanted to freshen up at the break. It wasn't unusual for Packer players to change their uniforms at halftime, but they had always made it a point to get back to the field in time for the action to resume. Coach Mike Holmgren was able to smile about Howard's tardiness after the game, but he didn't think it was the least bit funny at the time.

"Mike went ballistic," said tight end Mark Chmura. "He was as mad as he could be at a guy who'd had an unbelievable first half. It wasn't a screaming tantrum. It was more like Mike's head was going to pop. You know how his face would just turn beet red. But the coaches caught more of the brunt of his anger than Desmond. He just got a little Brett tantrum."

Holmgren didn't stay mad long, though, because the Packers drove 72 yards in 7 minutes and 54 seconds on their next possession and scored when Antonio Freeman recovered Edgar Bennett's fumble on the goal line. Chris Jacke's extra point restored a two-touchdown advantage for Green Bay, and the 49ers were barely heard from again as they turned the ball over four times in the second half and finished the day with only 196 yards of total offense.

The Packers ran 12 plays in their game-turning drive, and only two of them were passes. Bennett finished the game with 80 yards and two touchdowns rushing, and Dorsey Levens added 46 yards on the ground as the Packers made the most of the muck that they were so accustomed to.

"I think we came back to work on Wednesday, and we still had mud under our pads and shoes," said center Frank Winters. "You'd step on the ground, and it was like a suction cup. We knew in those conditions that the team that runs the ball the best is going to come out on top. Dorsey just wore people down, and they always talked about Edgar like one of those horses that runs in the mud. It was kind of weird for a guy from Florida to come up to Green Bay, and it seemed like he always played well in these conditions.

"If you got ahead, the chances of the other team coming back were going to be pretty slim. It was miserable to throw the ball."

It was especially miserable for the 49ers because Steve Young, their five-time NFL passing leader, had to watch from the sidelines after their first two drives. Young had cracked two ribs in the Niners' wild card game the previous week in Philadelphia, and there weren't enough painkillers in all of San Francisco to keep him on the field beyond nine plays. The quarterback wasn't the only Young who had to leave the game, and the other one's absence was almost as expensive for the 49ers. All-pro defensive tackle Bryant Young was taken off on a stretcher with a neck injury in the first quarter, and he never came back. Bryant Young had registered 11½ sacks that year and been named Associated Press first-team all-pro.

Elvis Grbac replaced Steve Young and found himself playing catch-up most of the day. He was forced to go to the air 36 times compared to Brett Favre's 15. It didn't help him to have the Packers paying special attention to his favorite target. Jerry Rice, the Niners' Hall of Fame-caliber receiver, had five catches that netted only 36 yards.

"We had a system called 'Mug 80,' which was kind of like a box and one in basketball where one guy follows Rice around and another guy plays zone behind him," said safety LeRoy Butler. "'Mug' was like we were mugging him. Fritz (defensive coordina-

Above: Brett Favre leads his grimy teammates off the field at the end of the first half.

Below: San Francisco fullback William Floyd finds Gilbert Brown to be a load.

tor Fritz Shurmur) threw out everything we'd been doing, so San Francisco couldn't see any of this stuff. It was the best game plan we had in my whole career.

"We put Wayne Simmons all over Brent Jones, and we put Craig Newsome all over Rice. Anywhere they went, they had help. If the 49ers ran the ball, it turned into an eight-man front. We were going to be aggressive at the line of scrimmage, and it didn't matter if Rice got by you because you'd have help. It got a little confusing, but it worked to perfection."

It worked so well that the 49ers netted only 71 yards and four first downs while the Packers were piling up a 21-0 lead with 3:18 to play in the first half. Howard accounted for Green Bay's first two scores almost by himself. He made at least five people miss on his 71-yard touchdown runback less than 3 minutes into the game, and he almost got to the end zone again 7 minutes later before settling for a 46-yard return to the 49ers' 7. Favre found Rison on a 4-yard touchdown pass two plays later.

The 49ers had come into the game with the league's fourth-ranked punt coverage team, but they weren't ready for Howard. Nobody was ready for Howard that year. He ran three punts back for touchdowns, and he set a league record with 875 punt return yards. Washington and Jacksonville had given up on him after he'd been drafted fourth overall in 1992, and the Packers signed him as a free agent in July.

"Desmond never said, 'I'm going to be an all-pro receiver,'" said Butler. "He just said, 'I can return the ball, and anytime I've got it I'm going to make something happen.' He would tell our special teams guys, 'I don't need you guys making great blocks. Just make good blocks and get out of the way. If we're side by side, don't even block the guy because we don't want any clips or blocks in the

back. If you can't get him, I'll take care of him.'"

Meanwhile, the Green Bay defense took care of the rest, helping to open a three-touchdown lead when Newsome turned an Owens bobble into an interception and ran it back to the 49ers' 15. Bennett scored three plays later. But then oddly enough, the Packers had trouble getting out of their own way. San Francisco punter Tommy Thompson's 30-yard shank hit Chris Hayes in the leg, and the 49ers fell on the ball at the Green Bay 26, leading to an 8-yard touchdown pass from Grbac to Terry Kirby. Hayes later atoned for his mistake by recovering a fourth quarter fumble that the Packers converted into their final touchdown.

By then it was just arithmetic. The Packers had been eating up the clock with their running game, and even when they weren't making first downs, they were gaining field position through the efforts of Hentrich. Green Bay's punter had three kicks downed inside the 20 while averaging 43.2 yards on six attempts, compared to Thompson's 35.8 yards. It was a notable performance coming from the middle of a mud puddle.

"Craig just had an even head on his shoulders," said place-kicker Chris Jacke, whose five extra points that day gave him the team record for playoff scoring with 52 points. "He didn't let things bother him. In our positions, you can't dwell on what's wrong.

"The field was such a quagmire, especially inside the numbers where they hadn't redone the sod. Several times the special teams coach came up and said, 'Can we kick this 40-yarder or 45-yarder?' And I said, 'There's just no way. Let's play field position and let Craig go out there and pin the ball down inside the 10-yard line.' It was a game of field position."

It was also a game of bragging rights for the Packers.

They had eliminated the 49ers from the playoffs the previous year, and they'd beaten them in the regular season, but the five-time Super Bowl champions still didn't seem convinced that the Packers were the better team until this match left no room for argument.

"It wasn't just that we beat them. It was how we beat them," said running backs coach Harry Sydney, who had played for both teams. "We ran the ball right down their throats. There is nothing more demoralizing than when a team runs the ball down your throat."

Not even missing the second half kickoff. Desmond Howard clearly demonstrated that.

Eugene Robinson returns one of his two interceptions.

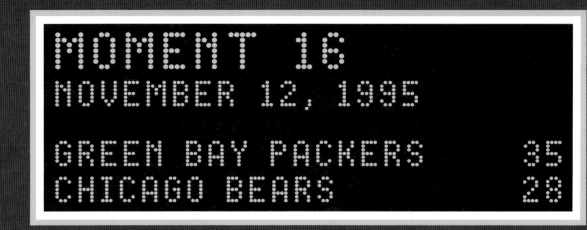

MOMENT 16
NOVEMBER 12, 1995

GREEN BAY PACKERS   35
CHICAGO BEARS   28

SHARING THE PAIN

The way Brett Favre describes it, his left ankle was purple and blue with a little yellow mixed in. Trainer Pepper Burruss took pictures. Burruss took pictures of almost all of Brett Favre's injuries, and this one was especially colorful.

The sprain throbbed all week, causing Mike Homgren almost as much pain as it did his quarterback. The coach was getting desperate. Favre had gone down the Sunday before in a maddening 27-24 loss at Minnesota, and he'd been replaced by Ty Detmer, who promptly tore a ligament in his right thumb. He was replaced by the unforgettable T.J. Rubley.

At least Holmgren would never forget Rubley. The third-stringer called an audible on a fourth-quarter play and threw an interception that eventually cost him his job and the Packers the game with the Vikings. And now the Bears were coming to town, and Holmgren was faced with the real danger of having to rely on Rubley again while Favre recovered.

He signed journeyman Bob Gagliano to take Detmer's spot on the roster, and there was even a report in the *Milwaukee Journal Sentinel* that he'd called 39-year-old Joe Montana to talk him out of retirement. Holmgren clearly did not want Rubley running his football team against Chicago in a crucial division match-up, but Favre had left Minnesota on crutches and hadn't practiced since.

Naturally, it was the Bears who were next on the schedule. They were 6-3 and winners of four of their last five games, while the Packers were 5-4 as was Tampa Bay. Coming up was the 150th meeting between Green Bay and Chicago and the most important in more than 20 years.

"The Rubley fiasco had Mike's ear until about Thursday," recalled tight end Mark Chmura. "The whole thing with Rubley in Minnesota was that he specifically went into that game not to check the play off. I remember it plain as day. Holmgren said, 'Whatever you do, don't check out of it.'

"So he starts audibilizing, and Frankie (center Frank Winters) starts screaming at him, 'Don't check out of it.' He checks out of it, throws a pick, and we lose. Mike was out of his skin, and we didn't want Rubley to play against the Bears. Especially coming off that loss. The big question mark was: Was Brett going to play?"

The answer didn't come until Sunday when Favre trotted out of the tunnel into a snowy, 22-degree afternoon and lit up the disbelieving Bears. Twenty-five pass completions, 336 yards and five touchdowns later, a reputation was made that would only increase over the next two decades.

"I think that game showed how tough Brett was," Chmura said. "That really was the start of it for Brett in our eyes."

Only Favre can say how close he came to missing Game No. 55 in a record streak of consecutive NFL starts, and only Favre knows

Brett Favre plants his injured left ankle and lets fly against the Bears.

how much pain it cost him to keep the string intact. He says that once the action started, the injury never felt better, and it never felt worse. His concern wasn't how much it hurt, but how much it limited what he could do.

He knew one thing for sure: the Packers needed him after what had happened with Minnesota and Rubley. It didn't help that Reggie White had injured his knee in that game, and it wasn't clear until late in the week whether he would play.

"For whatever reason, every time I've been hurt and had to come out of a game or stayed in a game, with for instance a broken thumb, the following game was a very difficult one against a team that was as good as or better than us," Favre said. "I didn't practice at all for the Bears. I was in the training room around the clock. Then Kurt (assistant trainer Kurt Fielding) would come over to my house at night and set me up with this ice pump. It's a big boot that swells and compresses. The next day, we would be doing all this stuff, and my leg stayed up the whole time.

"I told Mike on Saturday, 'I think I can play,' and he said, 'Fine, that sounds great. But tomorrow I've got to know what you can do or not do.' We treated it right up until the kickoff, and we had it taped like a cast. I wasn't worried about whether I was going to hurt it. I was worried about whether the way I play the game was going to be taken away from me. My game is all moving around and making something happen. I said to myself, 'This is going to force me to play in a

Round the clock treament on his injured ankle allowed Favre to start his 55th consecutive game.

Edgar Bennett takes off on a rare run. The Packers gained only 43 yards on the ground while Favre passed for 336.

Rashaan Salaam helps the Bears pile up 140 yards rushing.

different way, whether I like it or not. And I don't know if I can do it.'"

It didn't take him long to find out.

Erik Kramer threw a 21-yard touchdown pass for the Bears on the first offensive series of the game, but the Packers came right back with a seven-play, 59-yard drive capped by Favre's 17-yard screen pass to Edgar Bennett. Favre followed that with a 29-yard strike to Robert Brooks one play after Antonio Freeman returned a Chicago punt 26 yards. At that point, it was already becoming clear that the Bears didn't know what to do with Brooks, who went on to catch six passes for 138 yards and two touchdowns, or with Freeman, who piled up 132 yards in returns.

It was also obvious that the Bears were more interested in stopping the run than they were in pressuring Favre. Donnell Woolford, their best cornerback, was out with a thigh injury, and they lost starting free safety Mark Carrier in the first quarter with a sprained knee. Wary of exposing their lame secondary in man-to-man coverage, they rarely blitzed until the second half. The strategy did allow them to hold the Packers to 43 yards on the ground, but it also spared Favre's tender ankle.

Chicago finally changed its approach with 2 minutes to go in the second quarter, and sent linebacker Vinson Smith after Favre. He nailed him for a 13-yard loss, but Favre had thrown a third touchdown pass by then to Dorsey Levens. The teams were tied, 21-21, at halftime.

Kramer, who led the Bears to 444 yards that day or exactly double their average going into the game, directed them on a 68-yard third period march, but then the Packers got organized on defense. They shut down the visitors three times in the fourth quarter, and the rest of the story belonged to Favre.

Chicago did manage to sack him two more times, but he was able to exploit their single coverage with bombs to Brooks. The last of those covered 44 yards and tied the game at 28 in the third quarter. Then he found Bennett on another screen for 16 yards and the winning score with 9:17 to play. His fifth touchdown pass of the afternoon equaled a club record while surprising the Bears, the sellout crowd of 59,996 and himself.

"I wasn't able to play my regular game," Favre said. "It was never like 'roll to the left and roll back to the right.' I mean, I wasn't dead in the water, but there was no mobility whatsoever in my ankle. And that's probably where it started with me as far as ankle injuries and bone spurs are concerned.

"The following week, I practiced some, but it didn't just get better overnight. I kind of eased back into it. I'm as surprised as anybody that I had that much success."

The Packers went on to win five of their last six games to clinch the NFC Central Division title and ultimately move into the NFC championship round while the Bears never quite recovered from that game. They finished 9-7, a record that left them out of the playoffs, and spiraled downward from there during Dave Wannstedt's final three seasons as coach.

"You have to give Brett credit," said center Frank Winters. "He went out there and performed on guts. It's amazing to me. That's why he is where he is today, because of performances like that."

General manager Ron Wolf takes that a little further. "It speaks volumes about who he is," Wolf said. "There are probably 10 guys from Green Bay who should be in the Hall of Fame who aren't (in addition to the 21 who are), and you're talking about the guy who is now the best to have ever played in a Packers uniform."

The Bears were harder to impress that day. A number of them said at the time that they doubted that Favre was hurt all that badly. Smith, the linebacker who sacked him in the second quarter, was quoted in the *Journal Sentinel* as saying Favre's injury was something the Packers "cooked up."

"He's a good player, okay?" Smith told reporters after the game. "He's not Troy Aikman."

Smith's comments draw a deadpan response from nose tackle John Jurkovic. "He's not working in a scouting department, I assume," Jurkovic said. "You look back on it, and you just laugh when a guy says he's never going to be a player, and he turns out to be one of the greatest quarterbacks who ever played. It's almost comical."

Favre says it's only natural for opponents to be skeptical when someone overcomes adversity to have a big game. He admits to some of that himself. After all, it's hard enough for healthy people to play football.

"I don't know," he said. "I think I've played better under those circumstances than just normal circumstances. Don't ask me why. I wish I had the answer. If that's the case, I'd crack my ankle every week."

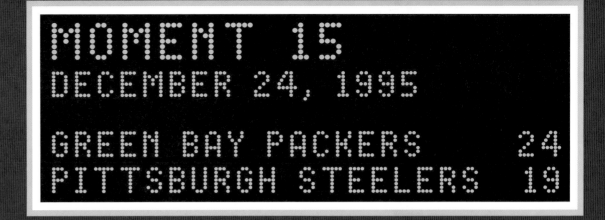

MOMENT 15
DECEMBER 24, 1995

GREEN BAY PACKERS   24
PITTSBURGH STEELERS   19

THE COMFORTS OF HOME

Yancey Thigpen was one easy catch from spoiling Christmas in Wisconsin, and Lenny McGill was at least 5 yards from doing anything about it. Standing all alone in the end zone, Thigpen needed only to snare Neil O'Donnell's perfectly thrown pass to win the game for Pittsburgh and end the Packers' hopes for their first outright division title in 23 years.

No one will ever really know why it didn't turn out that way, just as no one in the sellout crowd of 60,649 will ever forget what happened instead. While a badly beaten McGill watched helplessly, Thigpen let the ball slip through his hands, off his thigh pad and on to the ground. It was the mistake that began the mystique. After the Packers ran out the last 11 seconds of the game, they became officially unbeatable at home.

"I couldn't believe it," recalled general manager Ron Wolf. "I know Lenny McGill was covering Thigpen. Well, I guess you couldn't say he covered him, could you? He was so wide open. How do you explain that? That started the Lambeau Field mystique. We started getting that, and we kept it. We kept it the whole time."

The whole time amounted to 29 straight victories at home, counting four in the playoffs. The Packers had actually begun the streak in the third week of the regular season after losing their home opener. The triumph over the Steelers was No. 7 in the string, but it was the one that let everyone know there was something special about playing in Green Bay during the Wolf-Mike Holmgren era.

Holmgren, in fact, was determined to make it special. At his Monday morning press conference before the game, he

appealed to the fans to create the most hostile environment possible for the visitors. "I want Lambeau Field rocking like it has never rocked before," he said.

And rock it did all day long. Especially after Thigpen's stunning drop.

"When he dropped that pass, I thought, 'This is God's country,'" said safety LeRoy Butler.

And a joyous place it was. To most people, the Christmas Eve conquest of the Super Bowl-bound Steelers was an outright gift for the City of Green Bay, which had just gotten the Packers' entire home schedule after sharing it with Milwaukee for 62 seasons. However, many of the players didn't see it that way.

To them Thigpen's bobble was poetic justice, retribution for the game almost being stolen from them not once but twice. Early in the fourth quarter, rookie Antonio Freeman had returned a kickoff to the Pittsburgh 8, but the play was called back when John Jurkovic was whistled for holding the Steelers' Deon Figures. And then with 1:51 to play, Gilbert Brown appeared to stuff O'Donnell's fourth down quarterback sneak at the Green Bay 11, but the visitors got the first down with a highly controversial spot.

Jurkovic ventures no opinion on the spot, but he's crystal clear on the holding call. "I went to the sideline, and Mike Holmgren was mad. He was all fiery red," Jurkovic said. "(Special teams coach) Nolan Cromwell came up to me and said, 'Did you hold him?' I said, 'I raped him.' Did I hold him? I held him like there was no tomorrow. The guy made the right call.

"That was a tough game. They had a quality squad with good offensive linemen. It was just two heavyweights battling it out."

The Packers were relatively new to that weight class, having finished three straight 9-7 seasons under Holmgren with two wild card appearances but no division titles.

The Steelers' Carnell Lake puts a lick on Robert Brooks, who caught 11 passes for 137 yards and a touchdown.

Edgar Bennett picks up some tough yardage. Bennett gained 57 yards on 15 carries.

After winning five of their previous six games, they'd taken a 10-5 record into the match with the Steelers, but they still needed to win to clinch the division. The Detroit Lions had won the previous day and would have held the tie-breaker advantage over the Packers if the teams had finished with identical records.

The Packers also weren't sure they'd be at full strength. Eleven days earlier, Holmgren had announced that Reggie White would undergo surgery on his left hamstring and miss the rest of the season. But White had returned to practice the next day, and now he would be making his first start in three weeks.

The Steelers, who came to town 10-5 and on an eight-game winning streak, had injury problems of their own. Running backs John L. Williams and Bam Morris were both out, putting most of the offensive load on O'Donnell's shoulders. On this day, he proved to be more than equal to the task by throwing 55 passes and completing 33 of them for 318 yards and a touchdown.

Pittsburgh's four- and five-receiver sets were an all-day migraine for the

Packer defense, which surrendered a total of 398 yards and once again failed to come up with a single turnover. Green Bay had the league's least opportunistic defense that year with only 16 takeaways.

Brett Favre helped compensate for that shortcoming with a club record seven 300-yard passing days. This was one of them. He went 23 for 32 for 301 yards and two touchdowns.

His first touchdown came on a 19-yard pass to Robert Brooks with 1:56 left in the first half, and it gave the Packers a 14-3 lead. But then O'Donnell exposed Green Bay's deficiencies on pass defense when he took the Steelers 70 yards in 96 seconds to make it 14-10 at half-time on an 8-yard touchdown pass to Ernie Mills.

But the Steelers' aerial game wasn't infallible. It was a dropped pass that helped Green Bay get field position on the Pittsburgh 32 and set up Favre's 1-yard scoring strike to Mark Chmura early in the third quarter. Favre had to call time out on the play before the touchdown when he was leveled by safety Myron Bell and Greg Lloyd, the same linebacker who'd been fined $12,000 for a hit on Favre in the pre-season.

"That was the year that Lloyd just absolutely drilled Brett," Chmura said. "So we knew what kind of team that was."

It was obviously the resilient kind as the Steelers came right back with a 72-yard drive that ended in another Norm Johnson field goal and cut the Packers' lead to 21-13. Chris Jacke returned the favor with a 47-yard kick for Green Bay, but then O'Donnell took Pittsburgh on another long march that Tim Lester capped with a 2-yard touchdown run, making the score 24-19. The Steelers replaced O'Donnell at quarterback with the mobile Kordell Stewart when they went for the tying two-point conversion, but Stewart's pass was knocked down by Craig Newsome. The intended target? None other than Yancey Thigpen.

Jurkovic's hotly debated holding call came on the ensuing kickoff. "I was in on Figures, but he spun out, and when he spun out you could see my hand," Jurkovic said. "I was still inside my frame, which isn't holding in theory, but when he spun out, it looked real bad, and they ended up throwing the flag."

When they did, the Packers ended up on their 29-yard line, and they got no closer than Pittsburgh's 40 before Craig Hentrich punted into the end zone. The Steelers proceeded to eat up 5 minutes and 11 seconds of the clock in 19 plays to set the stage for Thigpen's final drop. The drive could have ended when Brown stacked up O'Donnell on the sneak, but the spot went Pittsburgh's way after a delay of almost a minute while referee Jerry Markbreit got down on his hands and knees to look at the measurement.

Seven plays and two timeouts later, Pittsburgh was lined up in a shotgun on the Green Bay 6 with 16 seconds to play, and Thigpen was about to become famous in Wisconsin.

He was already semi-famous in Pennsylvania after getting picked up by the Steelers as a street free agent in 1992. He became a Pro Bowl player and Pittsburgh's leading receiver in 1995 with a club record 85 catches.

As O'Donnell took the snap, Thigpen ran a slant on the left, isolating McGill on him and creating panic among the Packers who were watching the play develop. "We were on the sidelines seeing Lenny McGill just getting beat on the slant, and then Thigpen took it to the corner," Chmura said. "The ball seemed like it was in the air for about 4 minutes. It was kind of one of those 'Oooh!' situations."

McGill slipped on the play and was at least 5 yards from Thigpen when the Steelers' wideout arrived at the northwest corner of the end zone. "The guy ran a slant and go, and I jammed him on the slant," McGill said in a *Milwaukee Journal Sentinel* story. "I don't know if I threw off his timing or what. He did the outside move, and the ball was behind him. He just dropped it."

It looked like McGill had simply gotten toasted, but Butler insists it wasn't as bad as it looked.

"No, that was just good execution by Pittsburgh," he said. "We'd been running some combination zones all day, and every now and then they worked to perfection. So they went a step further and said, 'Let's run some crossing routes.' Any time you run a guy in front of a guy, the one coming across can be wide open. It's just amazing how wide open he was. We almost couldn't believe it. I just know when that ball hit the ground, I thought, 'This is our day.' They should have won that game."

Thigpen certainly would have agreed with that. After the game, he told the *Journal Sentinel*, "I just short-armed it. I felt somebody close, and I just wanted to pull it in and make sure. But I pulled it in too quick."

And it hit the ground, providing a dramatic ending to the Packers' 23-year wait for a division championship they could call all their own. If anyone missed the significance of that, Butler would be happy to explain it.

"When I put that division championship hat on, I thought about 1990 when I got here and I thought I might never win a championship in Green Bay," he said. "We had a bunch of older guys on the team, and I saw no light at the end of the tunnel. I remember Mike Holmgren's first speech. Actually I heard two speeches. I'm one of the only guys who heard Mike Holmgren's first speech and Lindy Infante's last one. When Holmgren first got here, he said, 'We've got to win the division first. Don't even think about the Super Bowl. We've got to win the division, get home field and have people come up here and play in the cold weather and the wind and the rain and the snow in the playoffs.'

"On Lindy's last day, he said, 'Guys, I don't know if I'm going to be back next year, but we finished good … yadda yadda.' Then I came back, and there's this 6-5 guy talking about winning the division, and I'm going, 'Hello? How are we going to do that?' But he put the framework together, and we really believed everything he said. So winning that game against Pittsburgh meant a lot to the organization, and it meant more to the players. But it all could have come crashing down that day."

But thanks to Yancey Thigpen, it didn't.

Matt LaBounty attempts to run down the Steelers' Kordell Stewart.

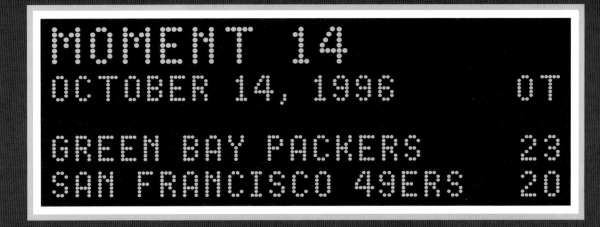

```
MOMENT 14
OCTOBER 14, 1996              OT

GREEN BAY PACKERS            23
SAN FRANCISCO 49ERS          20
```

A QUESTION OF RESPECT

Chris Jacke had something to prove as he stood 53 yards from the goal posts, and the rest of the Packers had a message in mind as well. They picked an ideal time to make their statements.

A Monday night audience was tuned in coast to coast to see if the Packers could reprise their 27-17 victory over San Francisco ten months earlier in the NFC divisional playoff round. Most of the viewers must have thought so because Green Bay was a six-point favorite, but many weren't convinced. Clearly among the doubters were the 49ers. But if the Packers could beat them back-to-back, it would be hard to argue that they weren't the real thing.

And now with 3:41 gone in overtime, it came down to Jacke, who had already sent the game into overtime with 8 seconds left in regulation. But that was with a routine 31-yard field goal. This was a dragon of a kick, and Mike Holmgren hadn't allowed Jacke to try to slay many dragons lately.

Jacke had gotten his season off to a bad start by missing three of his first 10 attempts. He'd also blown an extra point the week before in Chicago, and the coach was becoming more and more inclined to punt rather than have Jacke blast away from long range. In fact, he'd done just that earlier in the game from the same distance as Green Bay was facing now.

But he opted to go for three this time, and he would later describe it as his one really good decision of the night. Jacke made sure he felt that way.

The eight-year veteran had a lot of faith in his home run power, and when Holmgren decided to give him a shot, he

79

had to make sure he didn't waste the opportunity. He'd made four field goals that night including two that had created ties in the fourth quarter, and he was approaching the fifth calmly.

"Everyone asks, 'Do you get nervous?'" Jacke said as he looked back on the kick. "I think things happen so fast that you get in a zone. You're thinking about the spot. You're checking the wind obviously, playing in Lambeau Field. No you don't get nervous.

"On those kicks of 50 and longer, there's not a lot of pressure. You're going to make them only 50% of the time, so I didn't put a lot of pressure on myself. And I took pride in that I was successful more times than not from that distance. So I had a lot of confidence."

All of which was justified when Jacke boomed the ball through the uprights with room to spare, sending 60,716 people home happy and sending the visitors away grousing. When a team with a defense as touted as San Francisco's gives up 446 yards and six scores, you don't expect it to claim it has been robbed, but that's how the 49ers were talking when the game was over. Their complaint stemmed from the Packers' only touchdown.

They scored it in the third quarter on a busted play when Brett Favre hit Don Beebe 29 yards downfield, and Beebe got off the ground and ran 30 more yards to the end zone. Cornerback Marquez Pope insisted that he touched Beebe on the ground, and the play should have ended there, but the Niners lost the argument.

They also lost track of Beebe all night long, but then no one was expecting to see that much of him in the first place. He was called on to fill in for Robert Brooks, who suffered a season-ending knee injury on Green Bay's first play from scrimmage, and he

Holder Craig Hentrich (left) and Jacke celebrate.

Robert Brooks has to be helped off the field with a season-ending knee injury on the Packers' first play from scrimmage.

Beebe's 220 yards in receptions, including a 59-yard touchdown connection with Brett Favre brings the 49ers to their knees.

finished the night with 11 catches for 220 yards.

You could make the case that the 49ers lost one of the biggest games of the year to the two smallest players on the Packers' roster — Jacke and Beebe. Beebe, who stood 5-11 and weighed just 185 pounds, was more than compact. He was economical. An eight-year veteran, he'd signed with Green Bay for $300,000 as a free agent before the season began, and he became the team's third-leading receiver.

As it turned out, he chose exactly the right night to have the biggest clutch performance of his career. Both teams had just one loss going into the game, but the 49ers had been to the playoffs 13 times in the last 15 years and won five Super Bowls. The Packers had made it into the post-season three times in that span and won just one division championship.

"The 49ers were the pinnacle of the NFL," said defensive tackle Santana Dotson. "They were what everybody wanted to be. And rightfully so. It was a rite of passage that you have to go through the champs."

And that's exactly how it happened. The Packers finished the year at 13-3 to San Francisco's 12-4, giving them home field advantage throughout the playoffs. Which meant that when the teams met again in the NFC divisional playoffs, they did so at Lambeau Field. That game wasn't nearly as close as this one. The Packers prevailed, 35-14, and went on to win the Super Bowl.

There was no questioning their credentials once they'd done that, but it may have taken that long for San Francisco to get the memo. Asked if he thought the 49ers respected the Packers before that Monday night game, center Frank Winters said, "We really didn't think they did. They still had some of those older players. Jerry Rice was still there, and some good defensive players were still there. Early in the '90s, they and the Cowboys had won all of those Super Bowls, and we couldn't get over that hump. We knew when we played those guys, it was just going to be a dogfight."

81

they scored 17 points in the last 7:15 of the second quarter after falling behind, 6-0, on Jacke's first two field goals. They did it with a back-up quarterback, too. Elvis Grbac, filling in admirably for injured all-pro Steve Young, completed 21 passes for 182 yards and two touchdowns. The visitors were also missing tight end Brent Jones and fullback William Floyd, but the Packers wound up with some injuries of their own. They lost Brooks, offensive tackle Earl Dotson and running back Edgar Bennett before the game was over. Brett Favre called it the most physical game he'd ever been in, but then he may just have been worn out.

The Packers' quarterback threw a club record 61 passes, completing 28 for 395 yards, and three of them were nuclear bombs. He set up Jacke's first two field goals with a 50-yard heave to Keith Jackson and a 54-yarder to Beebe. But it was the 59-yard connection with Beebe that caused a major fuss. It came with 7:14 left in the third period, and after Favre found Bennett for the two-point conversion, the Packers had cut the difference to 17-14.

"That got us going," said tight end Mark Chmura. "When Robert blew out his ACL, we were kind of deflated and did nothing the rest of the first half. Then Beebs came out and went crazy. When he made that catch on the sidelines, I had the best view of anyone. I don't know if I picked him up or just started pointing and telling him to run. They said they downed him, but the ref never blew the whistle.

"From my angle Pope didn't touch him. He just went right over the top of him. I was right there, and I think I got over him and told him 'Go! Go! Go!' And then I just kind of got in the way of everybody else."

Pope was incensed, but the officials weren't interested in a debate, even if the ABC Monday night crew was. TV replays appeared to show that Pope touched Beebe before he got up. But there was no instant replay rule that season, and the 49ers had no recourse. They also had no answer for Beebe.

"Don had that ability to get hot," said general manager Ron Wolf. "He was the fastest guy on our team. Some games he showed up, some games he didn't. Thank goodness he showed up in that game."

The 49ers clung to their 3-point lead until Jacke's 35-yard field goal tied the game at 17 with 3:35 left in regulation, and then they took it again when Pope intercepted a slant pass and set up a 28-yard field goal that put them up, 20-17. Back came the Packers with a 10-play drive that took 1 minute and 42 seconds and moved Jacke into range for his tying 31-yard kick.

San Francisco won the overtime coin toss, but had to punt, putting the Packers in business at their own 44. Favre's 13-yard pass to Beebe helped them move to the San Francisco 35 and brought Jacke on the field one last time for the dramatic final play.

"I was snapping, and I was a nervous wreck myself," Winters said. "The pressure was unbelievable. I don't think Jacke got the recognition he deserved. You had people kicking in domes making like 33 of 35 field goals, and then you had Jacke making 29 of 34, but people don't take the elements into consideration. He was always a clutch kicker. I don't recall him missing many field goals at crucial times."

He didn't come close to missing this one, even though it was only one yard shorter than the longest field goal of his career.

"It cleared by quite a bit, and I knew it as soon as it left my foot," Jacke said. "If I had to say what the best kick of my career was, that would be it. Everything was perfect. As nervous as Frank was, the snap was right there, and Craig Hentrich did an excellent job of putting it down. I always say I have the easy part. They have the hard part.

"That was the high point of the season from an individual standpoint. And from a team standpoint, it seemed like we were always knocking heads with the Cowboys and 49ers. I remember doing an interview with Lesley Visser after the game and saying, 'We finally have shown up as a team that can play with the big kids on the block.'"

In the 49ers' case, the Packers not only played with them, they beat them five straight times from 1995 to the playoffs in 1998. Jacke's future in Green Bay, though, wasn't nearly as bright. He scored 820 points in his eight years with the team, but the Packers let him go in free agency after the season when he was just three points shy of Don Hutson's club record. Wolf and Holmgren were tired of his attitude and couldn't wait to get rid of him when the season was over, although some of the players were sorry to see him go.

Don Beebe has a lot to talk about with the press following an 11-catch performance.

"Can you believe that?" said safety LeRoy Butler. "I think it was that day and age when we were so good, why even pay a kicker? He was the kind of guy who was real quiet and to himself, and guys didn't really know a whole lot about him. I think he was demanding a little more money than they wanted to pay him, and the situation just wasn't right. But I would have loved to have seen him come back.

"Before the season, a lot of publications were saying that it was a fluke that we beat the 49ers in the playoffs, but we positioned ourselves to win that game with a good drive by the offense. And then Jacke made one of the biggest kicks of his career and the franchise's career."

Three months later, the Packers were winning the Super Bowl. They'd made their point.

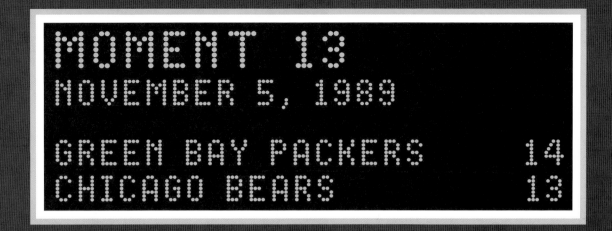

MOMENT 13
NOVEMBER 5, 1989

GREEN BAY PACKERS   14
CHICAGO BEARS   13

THE MAJIK OF REPLAY

It hardly seemed like the time for a chat, but Don Majkowski wasn't doing much anyway as Mike Singletary stopped by to have a word with him on a cloudy day at Lambeau Field.

Line judge Jim Quirk had just thrown a flag from half a field away, and the teams were preparing to take a 4 minute, 54 second recess while a man with a camera decided who would win their football game. The Packers' quarterback remembers being pleasantly surprised when the Chicago linebacker grabbed him by the jersey.

"I was walking toward the huddle, and he gave me a nice compliment," Majkowski said. "He said, 'That was a hell of a play. You had a hell of a game. But too bad. You're not going to win.' I said, 'It's not over yet.'"

Boy, did he have that right. The Hindenburg was consumed by flames in 37 seconds, or less than one-seventh of the time that it took replay official Bill Parkinson to make a decision that would change the rules of the game and give the Packers their most satisfying victory in almost a decade. And while Majkowski and eventually Parkinson disputed Singletary's conclusion, they could agree on one thing. It was a hell of a play.

The Packers were trailing the Bears by 6 points and facing a fourth-and-goal on Chicago's 14-yard line with 41 seconds on the clock when they lined up with four receivers and a plan to throw a slant pass. There was only one problem. The Bears were in the absolute wrong defense for the plan to work.

The play was designed for man-to-man coverage, but when Majkowski found the enemy in a zone he had no choice but to ad lib. Considering what had happened on his last two appearances inside the Chicago 25, he didn't look like the ideal candidate for that. He'd fumbled the first time, and then he'd thrown an interception to Ron Rivera with 7 minutes remaining in the game.

"Someone came on a blitz and hit my hand, and we almost blew the game," Majkowski said. "I heard some boos, and I felt awful. But what stood out to me was that Lindy grabbed me by the face mask as I was coming off the field and said, 'Just stay positive. Don't get down. You're still going to be the hero of this game.'"

Coach Lindy Infante would be called a genius before this season was over, but never a clairvoyant. But he got it right this time. Some 6 minutes after Majkowski threw a pass to the wrong man, he threw another one to exactly the

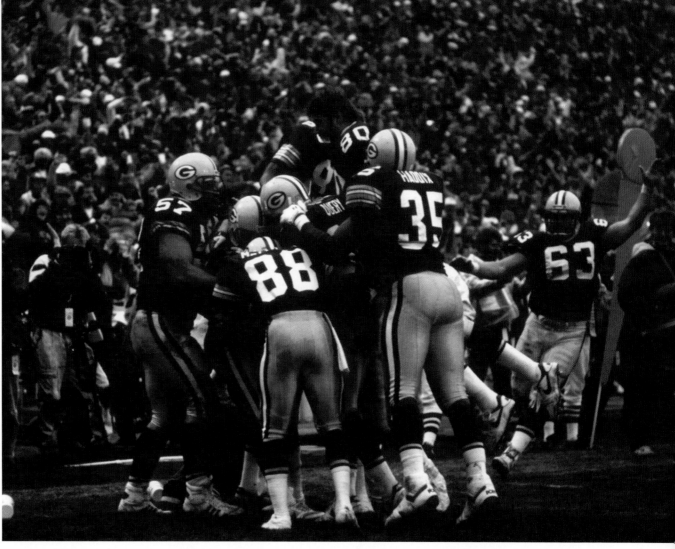

Sterling Sharpe is mobbed by his teammates after catching Majkowski's pass.

right man. Sterling Sharpe had caught only one ball all day, and that for just 5 yards, but he got to this one and took it into the end zone to tie the game at 13.

Sharpe would catch 90 passes in 1989, but Majkowski was never happier to see him catch a ball than he was this time.

"I totally improvised," he said. "Sterling Sharpe was split all the way out to the left. We were predicting that the Bears were going to all-out blitz us. They had blitzed me a lot in the red zone and had played man-to-man behind it. They figured they'd blitz us, and we'd throw a hot read — a short pass — and they'd come up and make the tackle. End of game.

"So we called a six-yard slant route to Sharpe, hoping that they'd be in man-to-man and that he'd catch it short and

Bears quarterback Jim Harbaugh and Mike Ditka pass the time as officials review the Packers' controversial touchdown.

break a tackle and go in. As soon as I got the snap they all dropped off into zone. A slant route isn't a great pass against a zone with that much yardage to go. So I got off Sterling and immediately started improvising. I looked around just trying to buy as much time as I could, hoping somebody would get open. It was a draw-it-in-the-dirt play."

Fortunately for the Packers, Sharpe had been reading the same dirt, and he came across the field to where Majkowski could see him. Unfortunately for the Packers, while Majkowski was finding Sharpe, Quirk was finding Majkowski, and the linesman decided that the quarterback had crossed the line of scrimmage before he let go of the ball.

Quirk threw a flag, canceling the touchdown, and the Packers called for the replay. What followed was 4-plus minutes of technology, uncertainty and angst. Working from the product of a stationary camera that had been mounted on the roof of the stadium, Parkinson played the tape over and over while 56,566 people fretted in the stands and the players stood around discussing the state of the union on the field.

The Packers of course were more than willing to wait. What were another few minutes after four years? It had been that long since they'd beaten the Bears, dropping eight games to them in that span while the Chicagoans were turning the NFC Central into private property. The Bears had won the last five division titles, but the Packers had reason to believe that times were changing.

Majkowski, a tenth-round draft choice who had

shared the starting job with Randy Wright in his first two years, was beginning to display the tools that would take him to the Pro Bowl, and Infante had brought a new attitude to a club anxious to emerge from the dark ages of Forrest Gregg. The team clearly thrived on excitement that year, winning four one-point games on the way to a 10-6 record, its first .500-plus performance since 1982.

That wouldn't be enough to get Green Bay to the playoffs, as Minnesota claimed the division championship on a tie-breaker, but it did give Infante a contract extension and the players a sense of accomplishment. Just beating the Bears was enough to give the players a sense of accomplishment.

"It was such a rivalry," said guard Rich Moran. "Forrest just kind of incited us, and it kept building and building. In '85 they beat us real bad, and they had a bunch of cheap shots on Lynn Dickey. Two weeks later, Forrest put together a highlight film of every cheap shot they made. That built the second game up to where Kenny Stills made that cheap shot on Matt Suhey, and then you had Charles Martin slamming Jim McMahon. I think everyone in the stadium would have loved to see Forrest and Ditka just square off at the 50-yard line."

But it was too late for that now. Gregg had been gone for more than a year, and Infante had weathered a 4-12 season before bringing the Packers into this game with a 4-4 record and aspirations of gaining some credibility by staying with the defending division champions. They'd gotten a good start on the credibility by taking a 7-0 lead into halftime on Majkowski's 24-yard touchdown pass to Clint Didier. But then the Bears had gone ahead, 13-7, on two Kevin Butler field goals and a two-yard run by Brad Muster.

The Packers were depending almost entirely on the passing game in the second half, running the ball just four times and throwing it 29. But Majkowski was getting constant pressure from the blitzing Bears, and his turnovers had stalled two drives. Green Bay was running out of time as it started its last possession on the 27 with 4:44 to play after a Chicago punt.

But then Majkowski drove the Packers 66 yards in 10 plays, giving them a first down on the Chicago 7 with 1:26 on the clock. They went backward in the three plays after that, losing 7 yards on two incomplete passes and a sack and leaving the outcome hanging on that one final, disputed pass.

"I was thinking it was going to be another one of those Bear games that we lost right at the end," said Moran. "As we waited for the call, I was just catching a rest and wondering what was going to happen. Not trying to be negative, but I was thinking, 'God, are we going to get this one turned against us?'"

Majkowski was feeling much more positive. After finishing his little talk with Singletary, he walked over to an official and told him that he couldn't believe the touchdown could be wiped out.

"We were just talking, waiting, kind of relaxed," he said. "I've looked at that play so many times since then, and my foot was a yard behind the line. I don't know where I released, but I think I was a yard behind the line of scrimmage."

It might have made Parkinson's job much easier if that had been true, but it really didn't make any difference where Majkowski's foot was when he let go of the ball. What mattered was where the ball was when it was released.

And referee Tom Dooley took great pains to explain that when he finally announced that Quirk's call had been overturned and the touchdown stood. The fans went nuts, and the players were pretty excited themselves. "It was euphoric," said Moran.

It was all of that, but Chris Jacke had a different memory of the situation, the kind that only place-kickers have.

"We tied the game," Jacke said, "but I still had to kick the extra point to win it. I remember thinking, 'Hey, we have one more play to go.' The eruption from the fans was still going on while we were kicking. It was incredibly deafening, but we had to go out and put the exclamation point on it."

When Jacke made the kick, the Bears organization came away with a different kind of punctuation in mind. The following year they listed the outcome with an asterisk, denoting "instant replay game" in their media guide. They did the same thing in their next nine media guides before finally dropping the subject in 2000.

The asterisk was the brain child of Bears President Mike McCaskey, who led a successful drive three years later to rid the NFL of instant replay. Some form of the rule had been in the books for six years, but it didn't come back until 1999. In addition, the league changed the rule on passes thrown beyond the line of scrimmage after Majkowski's wild run. What matters now is not where the ball is, but where the player's body is when the pass is released.

It was also reported in *Sports Illustrated* that Art McNally, the NFL's director of officials, eventually resigned because of the call. According to the magazine, McNally spent so much time going over the play in his mind that he knew he needed to get out of the business.

But the Packers didn't know about any of that when they learned that night that the replay had gone their way and they'd finally gotten the best of the Bears. Not that it would have mattered if they had.

"For me and for many of us who were part of the Packers organization throughout the '80s, when you talked to the fans the only thing they cared about was beating the Bears because we weren't a very good football team," said linebacker Brian Noble. "And to do it after eight games was pretty special."

Even if it took a little extra time to get it right.

Opposite page: Brent Fullwood looks for running room at right tackle.

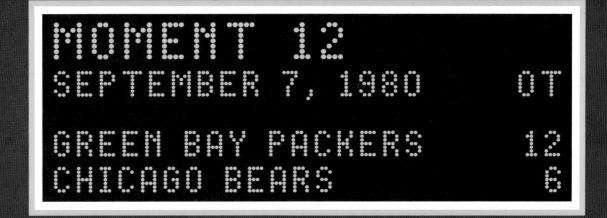

```
MOMENT 12
SEPTEMBER 7, 1980          OT

GREEN BAY PACKERS          12
CHICAGO BEARS               6
```

KICKBACK SCHEME

There had to be something in the water. In the week before the season opener, the opponents had been cheered at Lambeau Field on the same night that a customer had dumped beer on Bart Starr. The home team had been booed all the way into the locker room, and the star defensive end had been spotted wolfing down a hot dog on the sidelines. Four days later, the defensive line coach left in a huff and never came back.

Surely the football gods had used up the last of their wackiness on the Green Bay Packers. Well, not quite.

How about a touchdown run from the field goal kicker? In overtime. Against the Chicago Bears.

Though he stood 6 feet tall and weighed 200 pounds, bespectacled Chester Marcol was nobody's notion of a running back. But as he crossed the goal line with ball in hand like a man trudging home from the supermarket with a loaf of bread, it seemed weirdly appropriate that he should score the winning points in an unsightly upset. The sellout crowd of 54,381 didn't know whether to laugh or cheer, but after the week they'd seen, victory was cherished and form was optional.

Usually blocked kicks are a place-kicker's worst surprise, but Marcol wasn't shocked when his 34-yard attempt caromed off of Alan Page's face mask and back into his arms with 6 minutes gone in sudden death. "It was such a quick reaction, there was no time to get shocked until afterwards," Marcol recalled. "It was just a reaction to a play. Bang! There it was.

"The bottom line is that when a play happens that quickly, regardless of what play, you just have to react accordingly."

So Marcol turned left accordingly and covered the 24 yards to the goal line with nary a Bear in range, putting a tidy green bow on one of the messiest eight days in franchise history.

Like most things, it all began when something else ended. In this case it was the Packers' shipwreck exhibition season. A 38-0 loss to the Denver Broncos was the final straw in an 0-4-1 pre-season that saw Green Bay get shut out three times and outscored, 86-17. This coming in the wake of a 5-11 regular season — Starr's fourth losing year in five tries — that was eroding the head coach's popularity in a hurry. How bad was it?

Well, when the Broncos intercepted a Bill Troup pass late in the exhibition finale and ran it back for a touchdown, the

Jubilant Green Bay defenders surround Walter Payton after driving him out of bounds.

Wylie Turner intercepts a Mike Phipps pass intended for James Scott in the end zone.

fans cheered. And when the Denver score was wiped out by a penalty, they booed. And they were still booing when the team left the field. Later in the week, a roof was installed over the tunnel to the Packers' locker room. "I don't know who was in the stands," Starr told the *Green Bay Press-Gazette* at the time, "but the guy who poured beer and spit on me as I ran off the field I'd like to think is not one of our fans."

The offender was never identified, but it's safe to say that Dominic Olejniczak wasn't a suspect. The Packers

president stood firm in his support of the Packers' head coach all week long as speculation surged on Starr's future. Olejniczak said the club's Executive Committee had no plans to discuss Starr's status. His vote of confidence was about the only good news that Starr received all week. The air around him was becoming so toxic that he announced the cancellation of his regular Monday and Wednesday morning press conferences.

While the media was clearly becoming impatient, Starr believed the majority of the general public was still on his side, but that support took a big hit when reports surfaced of pro football's most infamous snack. In the second half of the Packers' debacle with Denver, defensive end Ezra Johnson was seen chomping on a hot dog on the sidelines. Defensive line coach Fred vonAppen was so incensed that he insisted that Johnson be suspended. It was a matter of principle, vonAppen said, and he didn't mean he was a vegetarian.

Starr had enough problems without sitting down his leading pass rusher, and he opted to fine Johnson and have him "voluntarily" apologize to the team instead. VonAppen wasn't impressed. Four days before the opener, he quit the staff.

"At the time, it was a big deal," said offensive lineman Greg Koch. "Did Bart support his players or did he support his coaches? But I think it was bigger in the media than it was on the team. Look at the problems today's players are having. Eating a hot dog on the sidelines is pretty minimal compared to that.

"Ezra was a very good worker. He always played hard. I think he regrets that he did it. We weren't playing particularly well, and eating a hot dog on the sidelines didn't

When Ezra Johnson downed a hot dog on the sidelines, it was more than defensive line coach Fred vonAppen could stomach. VonAppen is shown here during training camp.

look good. At the same time, it wasn't an offense punishable by being suspended for a year. Everybody overreacted a little bit."

Koch said that Starr just tried to mediate the situation, and it was hard to tell whether the coach's actions improved his standing with the players or not. But it seemed likely that coming down harder on Johnson wouldn't have made him popular with the help.

"We thought it was all bullshit," said linebacker Mike Douglass. "I never ate a hot dog, but I ate other stuff that might give me some energy. We were on his side. We just thought it was so overblown, especially for him. If it was some second string guy, it might have been different. But it was Ezra."

And it was Ezra in the starting lineup and defensive coordinator John Meyer as acting defensive line coach when the

Packers took the field against Chicago. The Bears were coming off a 10-6 year under Neill Armstrong and expecting great things. The great things never happened. They finished the season 7-9, but they were clearly favored over the Packers on this humid 70-degree day.

The Bears had Walter Payton for one thing, and they had a wily defensive lineman named Page, who was past his prime but who nevertheless would block 28 kicks during a 15-year career. That plus the extracurricular activities going on in the Packer camp appeared to be more than enough for Chicago to win.

"It always seemed like there was something going on," Douglass said. "We never had it smooth. We always had some kind of adversity going like that where we had to try to pull it together as a team."

And pull it together they did. At least defensively. The Packers held Payton to 65 yards on 31 carries with none of them going more than 9 yards, and they intercepted Bears quarterback Mike Phipps three times. The Packers' Lynn Dickey was having only a slightly better day with 10 completions in 22 passes for 138 yards with an interception. But the Packers' offense did produce one warm and fuzzy story in a week dominated by friction and frankfurters.

Larry McCarren had started 63 straight games dating back to the 1975 season, but his streak appeared to be doomed when he underwent surgery on August 14. Nobody hops off the table and plays center in the NFL after having a hernia operation three weeks earlier. Nobody but McCarren, who returned to practice on Thursday before the game and got the word from Starr on Saturday that he'd be starting.

"The plan was that he was going to play the first series to keep his streak alive," Dickey said. "There's not a normal person in America who could do that. And it was kind of a muggy day. I remember getting into the huddle about the start of the fourth quarter and 'Rock' is still there. I mean sweat is just pouring off of him. It looked like somebody poured a pitcher of water over his head. I said, 'Rocco, I thought you were supposed to get out of here.' He said, 'Just call the play, mister. Let's go.'"

Dickey called plays all day, and most of them didn't work. It was the same way with the Bears as neither team could cross the goal line. The Bears took the lead on Bob Thomas' 42-yard field goal in the first quarter and then Marcol came back with a 41- and a 46-yarder to put the Packers up, 6-3, at halftime. Thomas responded with a 34-yard boot to tie the game in the third quarter, and nobody scored in the fourth.

The game went into overtime. The Bears won the flip and elected to receive. Eight plays later, they punted the ball away, and the Packers were in business at midfield. Dickey connected immediately with James Lofton on a 32-yard pass, and after three running plays, Marcol was standing on the left hash mark just beyond the Chicago 24 hoping to end the game.

But Page had other plans as he sprinted into the Packers' backfield and took the kick on his facemask. Just as he'd predicted he would.

"Page was so close," Marcol said. "He confronted his teammates and told them, 'Don't worry, I am going to block this kick, so you guys had better watch it.' Alan Page was like Ted Hendricks when it came to blocking kicks. They were tall and lanky and very good at their trade. I'll tell you, when a kicker keeps his head down and kicks and sees the jersey of the opposite color in front of his face, he knows there are going to be two thuds."

McCarren heard both of them, and it was the last thing the sore and exhausted center needed.

"I probably weighed 230 pounds for that game," he said. "I hadn't been able to lift weights or anything. Thank God for shoulder pads, or the Bears probably would have laughed me off the field. When the thing went into overtime, I thought, 'Oh crap.'

"When they blocked the field goal, I think I was at least partially at fault if not all at fault because they got up the middle. Then I heard the double thud, and I thought, 'Oh no, this is going to go on.' Then Chester runs the thing in, and people are all happy. I was just happy the game was over."

The only one happier might have been Marcol, whose only previous opportunity to score an NFL touchdown had vanished the year before. David Beverly had underthrown him when he was wide open on a fake field goal attempt against New England. This time fate made a U-turn in his favor.

"The ball hit me right in the numbers," Marcol said. "It was right there. I didn't have to reach to either side. It was catch and run. Sometimes it makes a huge difference when a tenth of a second doesn't have to be wasted on reaching out for the ball. The game is so fast that a tenth or two-tenths of a second can make the difference between scoring or not.

"There was only one Bear jersey, and Jim Gueno either shadow blocked it or blocked it."

Either way, the Bears were done. Chicago would get its revenge on the Packers exactly three months later, blistering them, 61-7, at Soldier Field. Marcol meanwhile would be released just weeks after scoring his touchdown. Starr would last three more seasons even though the team won only four more games in 1980. He needed this one badly.

"It was kind of a cheesy way to win," Koch said. "But we took any game we could get."

Chester Marcol has his field goal attempt come off his foot (opposite page) and bounce back into his arms before he sets off for the goal line to score the bizarre touchdown that beats the Bears in overtime.

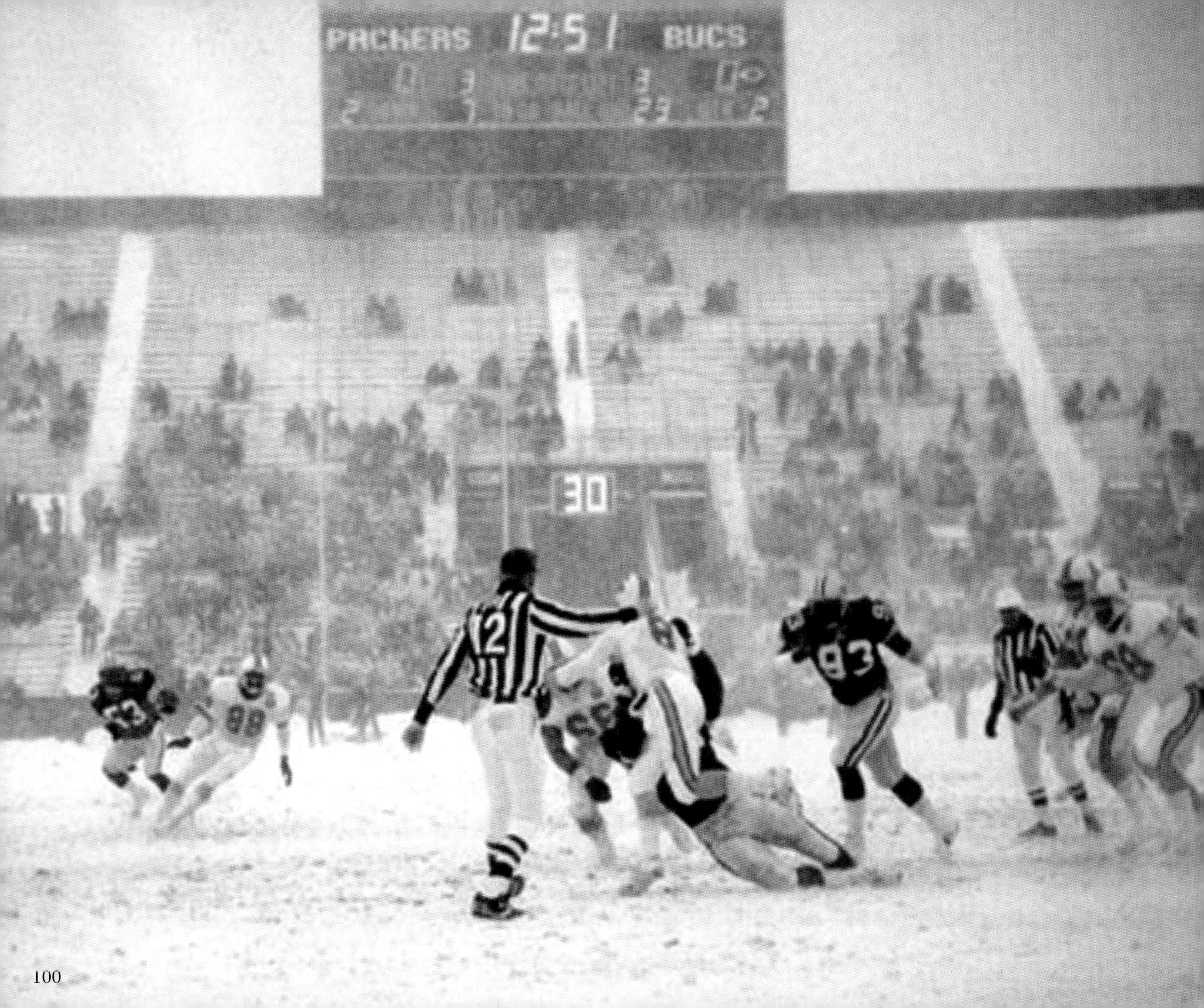
PACKERS
12:51
BUCS
30

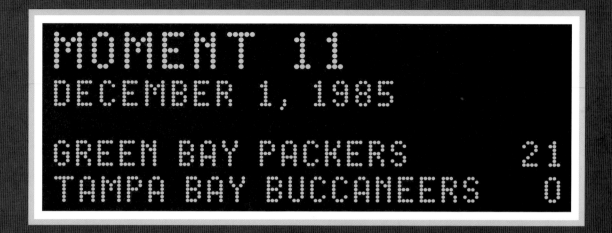

MOMENT 11
DECEMBER 1, 1985

GREEN BAY PACKERS 21
TAMPA BAY BUCCANEERS 0

SNOW BALL

The most powerful blizzard ever inflicted on a Green Bay Packers football game was blanketing Lambeau Field's mostly empty seats when Greg Koch had a little chat with Tampa Bay linebacker Scot Brantley.

The two teams were, to use the term loosely, warming up, and Koch happened to notice what Brantley had on his feet. Just like that, the Packers' tackle was sure the game was over.

"I knew we were going to win when they came out, and all they had was Nike Sharks," Koch recalled. "They had those rubber cleats that were only about a half-inch instead of the studded cleats that we had. The Sharks were great for very dry days on great grass, but if it was wet, they weren't worth anything because they wouldn't dig into the ground.

"I said to Brantley, 'You've got Sharks on. You're not going to wear those, are you?' He said, 'That's all we brought.' I told him, 'Whew! It's not going to be pretty for you guys today.'"

It was in fact downright ugly for the visitors as more than 10 inches of snow was getting blown around by 25 to 30 mph winds that day, and Packer quarterback Lynn Dickey was conducting a clinic in winter rules football. The Buccaneers and their Sharks found themselves swimming with the fishes as the Packers enjoyed one of their most impressive offensive performances under any conditions. The Bucs, on the other hand, would weather their worst.

How lopsided was it? Well, Dickey ignored the elements and threw 36 passes, completing 22 of them for 299 yards, including 6 to James Lofton for 106 yards. Running backs Eddie Lee Ivery and Gerry Ellis balanced the offensive load when both of them topped 100 yards, even though they carried the ball just 22 times between them. The Buccaneers

Greg Koch knew it was all in the shoes.

Lynn Dickey was right at home in the snow.

them to halfback James Wilder — and getting sacked 5 times.

"Lynn was a mudder," Koch said. "He played best in mud games and snow games, and they weren't going to get any pass rush on him because the defensive line-men couldn't get any footing. I knew Lofton and Lynn were going to have a field day."

Unfortunately, the fans were having a snow day. Blustery weather, slick roads and common sense kept more than 36,000 ticket holders from leaving their houses. The crowd of 19,856 was the smallest since Lambeau Field opened, and the players couldn't blame the stay-at-homes. They felt lucky to get to the stadium them-selves.

"Forrest Gregg had us staying at a hotel for home games," Dickey said. "When we got up for the pre-game meal, it was snowing pretty good, and it kept snowing harder and harder. A lot of the guys who drove regular vehicles couldn't get out of the parking lot, so they kind of doubled up with guys who had trucks and Jeeps to get over to the stadium.

"I don't think the grounds crew got the tarp off in time. It snowed so hard so fast that they couldn't pick it up, so they had to get the tractors with forks on them, and they just ripped the hell out of it and pushed it over

shattered a number of team records for frost-bitten futili-ty. Their 65 yards total offense, 41 offensive plays and 1.6 yard per-play average were all franchise lows, and their five first downs tied the club mark.

The Packers out-gained the Bucs, 512 total yards to 65, and they completely outmatched them through the air. Rookie quarterback Steve Young, who would go on to enjoy some success in San Francisco, spent all afternoon trying to get a grip on the ball and on himself. He never succeeded at either, completing just 8 of 17 passes — 6 of to the east side. The field already had four or five inches of snow on it, and I kept wondering if the Buccaneers were going to come out and play. I think I read in the paper that it was 83 when they left Tampa."

The Buccaneers did come out for warm-ups, but not until 40 minutes before game time. Leeman Bennett was in his first year as Tampa Bay's head coach, and things weren't going any better for him than they had for John McKay, the man he replaced. The 2-10 Bucs were on their way to a 2-14 season and pinning their hopes on Young, whom they'd lured away from the United States Football League. Those hopes were misplaced that day and for most of the two seasons that Young would spend in Tampa before moving on to the 49ers.

"Those guys just didn't want to be there," remembered linebacker Mike Douglass. "It was a very difficult game to play even for us. In all those cold games that I played in Green Bay, I always felt like my skin was coming off. It was so bad that day. It was wet snow and very thick. You got wet and stayed cold the whole game."

Except maybe for Dickey, who started the game hot and stayed that way. The Packers had their share of problems in '85, but quarterback wasn't one of them. Dickey led the team to an 8-8 season after a 3-6 start, and it was hard not to be impressed by the way he coped with the weather. After the game, Young called him "a great player," an assessment that Ellis shares to this day.

"You can't say enough about him," Ellis said. "He was a guy who could throw a football through the eye of a needle, and he had five guys who could catch a B.B. at night. He knew what velocity to throw it at, and he knew where to throw it, outside or inside. And he could read a defense

It took four Buccaneers to bring down running back Eddie Lee Ivery.

Only 19,856 fans braved the elements, but these two bundled up and enjoyed themselves.

103

like there was no tomorrow."

Dickey found the Buccaneers to be easy reading on the Packers' first possession of the game, but Lofton stalled the drive when he fumbled after making a 27-yard catch with a seemingly clear path to the goal line. That was followed by another reversal when Al Del Greco's 26-yard field goal attempt was blocked. But Dickey kept plugging, and the Bucs kept slipping and sliding.

Dickey scored on a 1-yard run in the second quarter, and Ellis took over in the third by returning the second half kick-off 40 yards and running 35 for a touchdown three plays later. It didn't matter that Del Greco missed a 25-yard kick late in the third quarter because the Packers came back with an 80-yard drive that Jessie Clark finished with a 3-yard touchdown run. With 9:52 to play the scoring was done, and the Packers had their first shutout in eight years.

After the game, the Bucs were comparing Lambeau Field to purgatory, and Bennett was saying they would have lost by more in good weather. Ellis tends to doubt that.

"I think in those conditions it would have been hard for anybody to beat us," he said. "We were kind of gunned up for that kind of weather."

Tight end Paul Coffman (82) catches one of his five passes for 62 yards.

Opposite page: Wide receiver Phillip Epps dives for, but just misses, a pass from quarterback Lynn Dickey. Bucs defensive back Jeremiah Castille is at left.

105

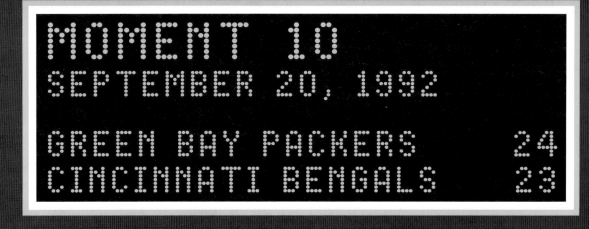

MOMENT 10
SEPTEMBER 20, 1992

| GREEN BAY PACKERS | 24 |
| CINCINNATI BENGALS | 23 |

BABY STEPS

Nothing's impossible, but this was way beyond unlikely and edging toward incredible. The Packers had 1 minute and 7 seconds to cover 92 yards with no timeouts and a brash young quarterback who kept getting knocked down and dropping the ball.

On the surface, it was just another game between two teams that wouldn't make the playoffs, but what Brett Favre accomplished in five plays on this sunny, 70-degree afternoon marked the beginning of so much more.

"It was like seeing a baby born," nose tackle John Jurkovic said as he looked back on the 35-yard touchdown pass that beat the Bengals and climaxed the first of more than 30 game-winning drives that Favre would direct over two decades. "You never really knew if he was paying attention in practice. You didn't know once he got into a game what was going to happen.

"We were in a battle, going back and forth, back and forth. Then we got to the final possession and had to make a play. Who would have known that was going to be the beginning of one of the greatest careers ever for an NFL quarterback? It was great to be there in the infancy of it all."

If a Hall of Fame career really was born that day, it was one tough delivery.

Ironically, the man who would set new NFL standards for durability got his chance only because of an injury, and he was making the least of it until that final drive.

The injured party was Don Majkowski, who had been struggling since his Pro Bowl season in 1989. Mike Holmgren had yanked Majkowski from a 31-3 embarrassment at Tampa Bay the previous week, but he wasn't ready to make a permanent change at quarterback. At least not until Majkowski tore the ligaments in his left ankle on the Packers' sixth offensive play of the game when he was sacked by Wisconsin's own Tim Krumrie.

Enter the kid from Southern Mississippi. Favre had thrown exactly four passes in two games for Atlanta as a rookie the year before and completed none of them. He'd gone a respectable 8 for 14 for 73 yards in the second half against the Buccaneers, but that was just mop-up duty. And this, he thought, was just emergency relief.

"I didn't think it was a lot different from any other game that I'd been a back-up, the only exception being that

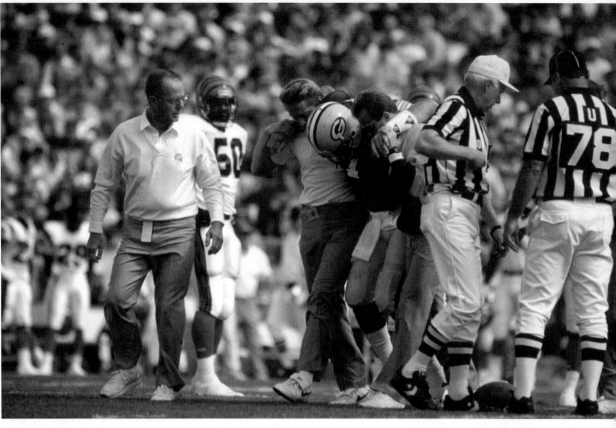

Don Majkowski is helped off the field with torn ligaments in his left ankle, making room for Favre in the lineup. Majkowski never started another game for the Packers after the injury.

I'd played a half the previous week," Favre recalled. "And that wasn't really a bring-us-from-behind type of game. It felt more like, 'All right, we'll just give him a chance and see what he can do.'

"So I really wasn't thinking I was going to play against the Bengals. I studied hard and prepared as much as I could, but the starter got most of the reps during the week — especially that year because Holmgren was taking over and the offense was new to everyone. Even though I was maybe their up-and-coming quarterback, he had to get Majkowski ready. Most of my knowledge came from watching or studying, and that's not the way I learn. I have to learn on the fly. I was familiar with the terminology, but putting the terminology with the play when people were coming after you was different."

And there's no question the Bengals were coming after him. They sacked Favre five times for a total of 36 yards in losses that day, and he also had four fumbles and lost three of those. Still, he'd managed to complete 18 of 34 passes for

197 yards and a touchdown before Green Bay's final possession, and so his self-confidence was intact. With Favre, that would always be the last thing to go.

The Packers started their winning march on their own 8-yard-line, thanks to a rookie mistake by return man Robert Brooks. Cincinnati had just taken a 23-17 lead on a 41-yard field goal, and the ensuing kickoff was headed out of bounds when Brooks grabbed it less than a yard from the sidelines and stepped out.

While 57,272 customers wondered what in the world he'd do next, Favre broke the huddle with almost 90% of the field in front of him and barely more than a minute to cover it. None of which seemed to bother him.

"I think he was calm," said fullback Harry Sydney. "Really, he had nothing to lose. He had the get-out-of-jail-free card. He was taking Majik's place, and nobody knew anything about him. At that moment in time, if he did well, great. If he didn't do well, he was replacing Majik, and as a rookie, we didn't know what he was supposed to do."

Technically, of course, Favre wasn't a rookie. He did throw those four passes for

Terrell Buckley is happy to be at the bottom of this pile after returning a punt 58 yards for a touchdown.

Atlanta in 1991, but Holmgren regarded him that way. He knew when Ron Wolf acquired Favre from the Falcons in February that he was getting a project. But Favre was a highly promising project, and if he panned out he might just provide the answer to a 20-year-old problem for the Packers.

Green Bay had tried 17 different starting quarterbacks since Bart Starr started his last game in 1971 and never found one who could lead a consistent winner. Lynn Dickey was the best of them, but he was immobile and susceptible to injury, and most of the rest were forgettable. Favre was anything but that, even on his worst days. He could be cocky, erratic, error-prone, brilliant and unpredictable, but never forgettable. And on this occasion, he was most of the above.

"The whole game was a mixture of mistakes and overcoming mistakes for me — an excellent throw, a sack, a fumble, a blend of everything," Favre said. "It wasn't like I overpowered the Bengals. It was just a fun game. I had numerous passes that could have been picked that weren't, and I had some throws that were maybe as good as any I've had in my career and some that were probably as bad as any I've had in my career.

"If the odds were ever against me, it would be in that game, but my feeling was, 'What the hell, everyone expects us to lose anyway. Here I am a back-up. I'm just going to turn it loose.'

"As I'm sitting here now looking back at it and trying to critique myself before that drive, I'm thinking, 'You were such a knucklehead. You thought you knew it all.' But I believe there's some merit to that. Sometimes, you just have to throw caution to the wind and look past the odds, and that's what I did in that game. Call it dumb, blindness, naivete, whatever. That's really the way it was."

His teammates didn't know quite what to call it at the time, but they were willing to find out. Green Bay had gone 10-6 with Majkowski in 1989, but then the Majik Man seemed to lose his magic. The Packers finished 6-10 in 1990 when he held out for most of training camp, and they were 4-12 the year after that when he missed six of the last seven games with a hamstring injury. For a team that had had only three winning seasons in the last 19, that was not a good sign.

"With the injury and the holdout and everything like that, it was kind of like, 'Oh, oh, here we go again,'" said linebacker Brian Noble.

It did look like it was time for a change, but a change to what? Asked what he remembered about Favre that day, Noble said, "Nothing, other than when he came out there he threw the ball like 100 fricking miles an hour. You knew he was good, but you didn't know how good. He was just a young kid that kind of approached things in a little different way than most people. He was kind of crazy."

This may have been the perfect game for Favre because it was kind of crazy, too. The Packers fumbled the ball seven times, while their quarterbacks suffered six sacks, and Chris Jacke, their normally reliable place-kicker, missed field goal attempts of 32 and 47 yards — partly because Favre had to fill in for Majkowski as the holder. They also gave up a 95-yard punt return by Carl Pickens for a touchdown, and when Cincinnati parlayed a Favre fumble into a 17-yard scoring pass from Boomer Esiason to running back Eric Ball they found themselves trailing, 17-3, with 1:31 to play in the third quarter.

But then they came back with 21 points in the final period. Terrell Buckley got the revival started by scoring on a 58-yard punt return of his own, and after the Bengals' Jim Breech made it 20-10 with a field goal, Favre threw a 5-yard touchdown pass to Sterling Sharpe to cut the difference to 20-17. Breech struck again to make it a 23-17 game with 1:07 to play and set the stage for Favre's climatic final drive.

He got 4 yards on first down with a swing pass to Sydney, and then he launched a 42-yard rocket to Sterling Sharpe, who made a spectacular catch but landed awkwardly. Favre followed that with an 11-yard completion to running back Vince Workman, and then he spiked the ball to stop the clock with 19 seconds to play. It was at that point that Sharpe left the game, having injured his ribs on the catch two plays earlier. Suddenly Favre faced the biggest play of his young career without his best receiver.

Kitrick Taylor celebrates his catch with Favre.

Replacing Sharpe was an itinerant wideout named Kitrick Taylor.

A fifth-year veteran who had caught just 33 passes playing for three different teams, Taylor came to the Packers as a Plan B free agent before the 1992 season, and he didn't stay long. He would play only 10 games in Green Bay before being waived in November.

"I can picture him like it was yesterday," Jurkovic said. "He was a strapping young fellow. But you had so many guys that came in and came out of NFL locker rooms from season to season. Hell, from month to month."

Although Taylor was just passing through, he was about to make a lasting impression. It was second and 10 when the Packers lined up at the Cincinnati 35 with four receivers and a familiar play.

"It was 'two jet, all go,'" Favre said. "I'll bet we still practice that play five times a day. It's been a staple in this offense and in my career. Of all the plays we have, especially back then, it's the one I really feel I can complete even when they've got it covered. It's just four verticals, and all I do is read the safety or safeties, step up and pump fake one way or another and just drill it.

"The safety got caught out of place that time. I pump faked, and if he hadn't gone for the pump fake, I probably would have thrown it inside. If he'd stayed inside thinking tight end, then I'd just drill it in the hole. I feel like I can overpower some teams or players with my arm, and I just thought if the protection held up, this would be a legitimate chance to score.

"When I let it go, my eyes lit up. I kind of had to put my left hand on the right tackle and sidestep him a little. The timing was not '1, 2, 3, 4, 5, hitch, throw.' It was '1, 2, 3, 4, 5, hitch, scoot to the left a little bit and then kind of reset and throw.' When I reset, I knew he was wide open. It was like, 'Oh boy, if I make the right throw, it's going to be a touchdown if he catches it.'"

Favre made the right throw, and Taylor caught it in stride and raced across the goal line with 13 seconds to play for what would be his only touchdown catch in a career that spanned six seasons.

"I'll never forget blocking, and all of a sudden he throws this bullet down the right side," said guard Rich Moran. "I could not believe the velocity of that ball. I was thinking, 'You've got to be kidding me.' I'll never forget that pass."

Neither will any of the people who were at Lambeau Field to watch Favre throw it or the hundreds of thousands more who only wished they were. Wolf likens the occasion to the Ice Bowl as he recalls a Packer alumni night held after the game when broadcaster Ray Scott served as master of ceremonies.

"Ray said that 20 or 30 years from now there would be 400,000 people claiming they were in attendance for the pass from Favre to Kitrick Taylor," Wolf said. "I don't know how many people were at the Ice Bowl, but I've met at least 100,000. Ray said this was going to have the same impact, and he was right. He hit that nail right on the head."

There would be meetings between Wolf and Holmgren on the future of their young quarterback, but Wolf said that after the Cincinnati game there was never any chance that Majkowski would get his starting job back. He knew that, and Holmgren knew that, but the one man who didn't know it was Favre. Holmgren didn't want his young quarterback taking anything for granted.

"Mike didn't call me right in the first thing the next morning," Favre said. "We may have talked on Monday afternoon, but it wasn't anything like, 'Okay, now you're our starter. You earned it.' They kind of kept me hanging, and I think maybe he wanted to see how I responded.

"I knew I made some mistakes in the game, but I battled and gave us a chance to win and then pulled it out in the end. So I said to myself, 'Just bide your time. If it's next week, great, but I think you're in a perfect position.'"

It was next week. Favre led the Packers to a 17-3 victory over Pittsburgh seven days later and began a league record streak of consecutive starts by a quarterback. The number was at 237 games going into the 2007 season, and no one applauds that more than Majkowski.

"When I got hurt, I was thrilled that we won the game," Majkowski said. "I was down in the locker room getting treatment and watching it. I knew in camp that the guy had a phenomenal arm. And to watch what he's done over his career has made it a little easier to see that the guy who replaced me is one of the best of all time. That's pretty darn cool."

And it all began with one astonishing drive against the Bengals. Five plays and 54 seconds that will live forever at Lambeau Field.

Favre is his usually excitable self after completing his game-winning touchdown pass.

Opposite page: Vince Lombardi
gets a ride after winning his first
game as the Packers' coach.

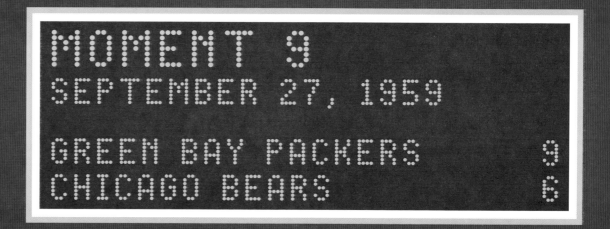

MOMENT 9
SEPTEMBER 27, 1959

GREEN BAY PACKERS   9
CHICAGO BEARS   6

GETTING CARRIED AWAY

His first game-day decision as a head coach had paid off big time, and now Vince Lombardi was getting a lift from the Packers. You might say they were returning the favor.

Not even Curly Lambeau had ever been carried off by his players, and he'd coached the Packers for 29 years. Lombardi would coach them for nine, but it was almost as if the players could tell what was coming as they put him on their shoulders after stunning the Bears in their season opener.

When Lombardi was hired to be the Packers' fifth head coach in January, he introduced himself by saying that he'd never been on a losing team, and he didn't intend to start with this one. The eyes in the room had barely stopped rolling when he set about replacing Scooter McLean's day care regime with his own maximum security approach. And now the results were there for everyone to see.

By scoring 9 points in the last 8 minutes on a Chicago team that had finished second in the Western Conference the previous year, the Packers served notice that they were a very different group from the one that McLean had allowed to wander through a 1-10-1 season in 1958. Or from the 10 before it that had all posted losing records.

Lombardi wasn't just providing temporary relief, either. The Packers would go on to win their next two games and finish the season 7-5, giving them a third place tie in the conference when everyone expected them to finish last.

And they were just getting warmed up. Lombardi never did have a losing team in Green Bay. What he had instead were five NFL champions and two Super Bowl winners. None of the players were predicting anything like that following the

Defensive end Jim Temp, a native of La Crosse and former Wisconsin Badger, played for the Packers from 1957-'60. He later served on the franchise's executive committee.

Lamar McHan got the nod over Bart Starr as the Packers' starting quarterback against the Bears.

Dave Hanner wasn't fond of grass drills, but they paid off when he clinched the victory with a safety.

ambush of the Bears, but they all knew that things would never be the same.

"His first meeting may be the most vivid memory I have of him," recalled Bart Starr. "He called in about 10 or 12 offensive players (in the off-season), and he opened the session by thanking the Green Bay Packers for the opportunity to become their coach. Then he walked right up to us and said, 'Gentlemen, we're going to relentlessly chase perfection, knowing full well that perfection is not attainable. But we're going to relentlessly chase it because in the process we will catch excellence.'

"He paused for a moment and got up right in our faces and said, 'I'm not remotely interested in just being good.' Well, God almighty, we didn't even need a place to sit. We were all up on the edge of our chairs. About 40 minutes later, we took a break, and that's when I ran downstairs and called my wife. I said, 'Honey, we're going to begin to win.'"

Starr was speaking collectively, but he could have been talking about himself as well. There was a quarterback derby in Lombardi's first pre-season, and Starr finished no better than second to veteran Lamar McHan. He may even have finished third to Joe Francis. Starr had played quite a bit in 1957 and 1958, but he'd never won a game as a starter, and Lombardi had his doubts about the young man's leadership qualities.

But when McHan injured his leg, Starr started the last five games of the season and won four of them. McHan got his job back the following season, but lost it to Starr permanently after struggling in Game 5 against Pittsburgh. He compounded his problems when he confronted Lombardi in a restaurant after the game.

"Bart was in a position where the head coach didn't think he was the guy," recalled tight end Gary Knafelc. "So they brought in McHan from the Cardinals. Physically, he was a fantastic quarterback, but he was

Intensity was never a problem for Lombardi.

117

emotionally unstable. He was a psycho. He'd get mad and do bad things."

Interrupting Lombardi's dinner was certainly a bad thing, particularly when the coach was constantly looking for ways to upgrade his lineup. Nobody's job was safe with him, a fact that he made abundantly clear by dumping five established veterans in his first seven months in office, including end Bill Howton, who was probably the team's best player at the time.

It was also alleged by a number of players that Lombardi had ejected team President Dominic Olejniczak from not one but two rooms. On one occasion, it was a meeting room at the St. Norbert College training camp, and on the other, it was the locker room.

If Lombardi was cantankerous with his boss, he could be downright sadistic with his players. At least three of them were fined $250 apiece before they even hit the practice field for the first time.

"Max McGee and I, and I think it was Howie Ferguson, checked into the dormitory for training camp a couple of days before the first meeting and then went out on the town," said cornerback Jesse Whittenton. "He fined us right in the general meeting when he introduced himself on the first day. Max said, 'Coach, camp didn't start until today.' But he said, 'It started the day you checked into the dormitory.'"

This kind of thing came as a major shock to the players who had gotten used to McLean's chummy approach. Defensive end Jim Temp said McLean never did get the team's respect. After all, that's hard to do when your poker buddies are your players.

"Early in training camp, Lombardi put Hawg Hanner in the hospital two different days from heat exhaustion," said Temp. "He ran a drill that he just relished. He'd walk around with all of us standing up, and then he'd say, 'Down,' and you'd go down on the ground. Then he'd say 'Up.' Then he'd say, 'Down.' Then he'd say, 'Right.' Then he'd say 'Left.' After wearing full equipment for a scrimmage, by the time you got done, you could hardly get up. Those grass drills were brutal."

But they were also effective. Knafelc said the Packers were a confident team the week before the opener with Chicago despite their sorry record the year before. Practices had been very precise, and the players knew what they were doing. Knafelc said one of Lombardi's techniques was to call players up to the chalkboard and have them diagram not only their own positions but the positions around them on certain plays against certain defenses. He kept people mentally fit that way. The grass drills kept them physically fit.

"I still maintain that we were in the best shape of any team in the National Football League, and it was all due to him," Knafelc said. "We all felt if the game was even in the fourth quarter, we were going to win it. Or even if we were behind by as much as two touchdowns, we were still going to win because we were in such good physical shape."

They were down only six points in Lombardi's debut against the Bears, and that was their own fault. McHan had struggled all day, completing only 3 of 12 passes for 81 yards, and a combination of bad throws, dropped balls, fumbled snaps and missed field goals had allowed the Bears to hold on to a 6-0 lead built on two field goals. Chicago had made it inside the Green Bay 30 just once, but the Packers still badly needed a break to upset the Bears.

They got it when Richie Petitbon fumbled to Jim Ringo on the Chicago 26, and five plays later Jim Taylor scored from the 5. Paul Hornung's conversion gave Green Bay a 7-6 lead, and after an exchange of punts the Packers padded that with the help of a decision their new coach had made almost three hours earlier.

The Packers had won the opening coin flip, and when Lombardi felt a 25 mph wind gusting out of the southwest on a rainy afternoon, he elected to kick off so that the gale would be on the home team's side in the fourth quarter. McGee took maximum advantage of the elements by booming a punt 61 yards. The ball rolled out of bounds at the Bears' 2, and on the next play quarterback Ed Brown dropped back into the end zone to pass. That's when

Lombardi is flanked by his first staff (from left) Phil Bengtson, Bill Austin, Norb Hecker and Red Cochran.

Hanner became the beneficiary of all those grass drills.

The veteran defensive tackle had dropped 18 pounds in his first two days of training camp, and he didn't miss an ounce of it as he leveled Brown for a safety. "Nobody could move Hawg," said Hornung. "He was as strong as a bull and very smart. Good poker player, too."

With that play Hanner had clinched Lombardi's first big pot. Ray Nitschke recovered the Bears' onside kick, and the crowd counted off the last 14 seconds before a posse of Packers grabbed Lombardi and provided him with free transportation off the field.

It was the start of a long, happy ride.

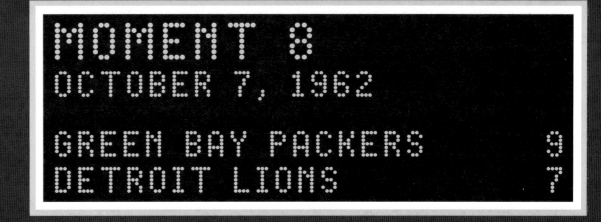

MOMENT 8
OCTOBER 7, 1962

| GREEN BAY PACKERS | 9 |
| DETROIT LIONS | 7 |

A PLUM ASSIGNMENT

Two franchises going in radically different directions collided in the slop at Lambeau Field, with the Packers on their way to a second straight world championship and the Lions headed for five decades of oblivion. It could have been fate, or it could have been just a brain cramp, but after Lions wideout Terry Barr slipped on this gloomy Sunday, Detroit never got up.

Barr, a solid receiver on a very good team, was chasing Milt Plum's what-was-he-thinking? pass when he lost his footing on the soggy turf, and Herb Adderley cut in front of him. The Lions' quarterback began the play by letting fly from midfield with 85 seconds remaining in what some say was the best regular-season game ever played in Green Bay, and he ended it by chasing Adderley out of bounds on his own 18-yard line. It was a signal moment in the history of both organizations.

Three plays after Adderley returned his interception 40 yards, Paul Hornung kicked a 21-yard field goal, and the Packers had taken their toughest step toward a 13-1 season. In the opinion of many experts, including a fair number of the players, this was Vince Lombardi's best team ever. But was it better than Detroit?

The Lions had the NFL's top-ranked defense, with the Packers ranked second and nobody else even close. Alex Karras and 300-pound Roger Brown anchored what Lombardi called the best front four in the league, while middle linebacker Joe Schmidt, cornerback Dick "Night Train" Lane and safety Yale Lary were destined for the Hall of Fame. Detroit's offense was a pale shadow of its defense, but the Lions did have Plum, whom they'd picked up in a trade with Cleveland after he'd

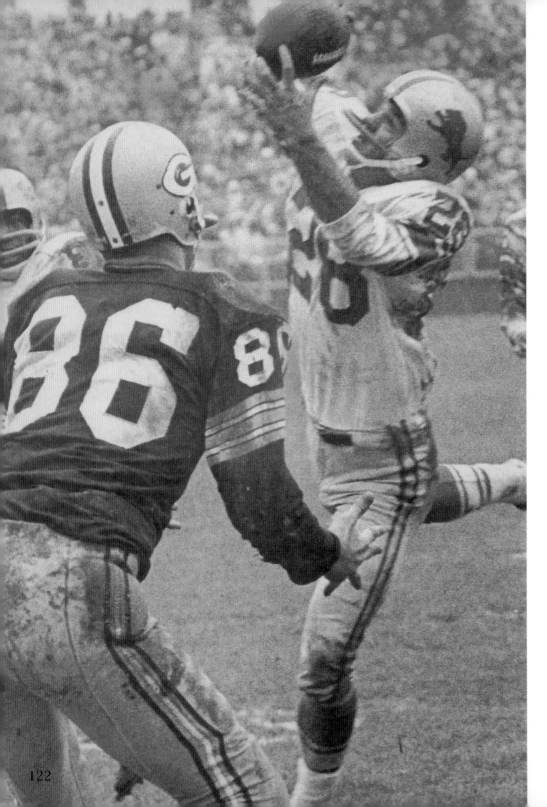

Detroit's Yale Lary picks off Tom Moore's option pass intended for Boyd Dowler.

led the NFL in passing in 1961.

The two clubs met again in Detroit on Thanksgiving Day, and the Lions were still mad enough to sack Bart Starr nine times in a 26-14 victory that was even easier than the score made it look.

"I remember the game in Green Bay like it was yesterday," said the Lions' Brown. "As far as we were concerned, it was a death nail. It just ticked us all off. We threw a pass to Terry Barr, and he slipped on the turf. It was like going from the penthouse to the outhouse in two seconds. If we had gotten ticked off every game the way we did on Thanksgiving in '62, we could have won some of those big games."

Instead, they finished in second place with an 11-3 record after losing their finale to Chicago when their title hopes were all but gone. But if they had hung on at Lambeau Field, they might have been the ones living on the top floor, and the '62 Packers might have been the best team that never won a championship. Fifty years have passed since the Lions last claimed an NFL title, and this may have been their best chance to break out of that drought.

"The '61 and '62 Lions were the best second-place teams you could ever come up with," said Boyd Dowler, who caught three passes for 45 yards that day at Lambeau Field. "They were a little shy on offense, but they were a good team. Their front four rush guys just gave us a lot of trouble. They came closer to stopping us than anybody ever did. And if they got it going on offense, they could beat us."

The Lions never came close to getting it going on offense when the two unbeaten clubs met at Lambeau Field for the fourth game of the season. They gained 199 yards compared to the Packers' 319, and their only score was set up when Karras jarred the ball loose from Starr on the Packers' 34-yard-line in the second quarter. Danny Lewis, a product of the University of Wisconsin, ran 6 yards for the touchdown, and Detroit never could get closer than field goal range after that.

But the Lions' defense was as dominant as their offense was feeble, a common occurrence that tended to cause friction in the locker room. "We were always upset with the offense," Brown said. "We called them the 'cha-cha-cha offense.' One, two, three, kick. One, two, three, kick. We spent a lot of time on the field."

On this occasion, it was time well spent. The Lions recovered two Packer fumbles and intercepted two halfback passes while holding Green Bay without a touchdown for the first time in 36 games. Starr was having a good day with 198 yards on 18-of-26 passing, and Jim Taylor managed to rush for 95 yards even though he'd been running a 101-degree fever the night before. But the Packers kept tripping over their turnovers, and they wouldn't have gotten on the scoreboard at all if Hornung hadn't booted a pair of 15-yard field goals in the first and third quarters.

The whole afternoon was about kickers. Detroit's Wayne Walker had a 25-yard attempt blocked by the ubiquitous Adderley in the second quarter, and he missed a 41-yarder in the fourth. Hornung was low and short from 47 yards in the final period, and when Pat Studstill returned his miss to the 22 with 6:01 to play, the Lions had the ball and time on their side.

What the Packers had on their side was Adderley and most of the sellout crowd of 38,669. But not all of it. When the Lions picked up a first down on their 47

Herb Adderley grabs Detroit quarterback Milt Plum's pass and takes off on a 40-yard run that sets up the decisive field goal.

with 2 minutes to play, hundreds of customers started heading for the exits. It might have been a good idea for Plum to do the same thing.

The Packers burned timeouts stopping the clock on the next two plays, leaving them with only one as the Lions broke the huddle facing a third and eight with 1:25 left in the game. A run and a punt seemed like the only logical plan for the Lions, given the way their defense had been playing all year. But it didn't seem that way to George Wilson.

Detroit's coach insisted that he and he alone made the next call. "We were just going for the first down," he told the *Green Bay Press-Gazette* after the game. "And remember, we had made two in a row on the same play. Supposing we had kicked the ball? They complete a long pass and kick a 35-yard field goal."

A gloomy supposition that turned Adderley into a hero for one of the first of many times. The Packers had drafted the Michigan State star in the first round in 1961 without a clear idea of how to use him. They tried him at running back and they tried him at flanker, but then he found a home when they moved him into the secondary to fill in for the injured Hank Gremminger on Thanksgiving Day in 1961 and he intercepted a pass. During his nine years in Green Bay, Adderley intercepted 38 more passes and set a franchise record by returning seven of them for touchdowns, establishing an enduring reputation for coming through in the clutch.

"Herb was our big play guy," said safety Willie Wood. "He had a knack for it."

There weren't many bigger plays than the one that ended this epic battle with the Lions, and few more surprising.

"I was a little bit shocked," said Dowler. "They were ahead, and they threw a square-out pattern, which is a dangerous type of throw anyway. You've got Herb sitting back there ready to jump on it like a cat. I don't think it was a very good call, but if you execute it, it's good."

It was Adderley who did all the executing when Barr slipped and he picked off the ball and ran it back to the 18. Describing the play to Bob Wolf of *The Milwaukee Journal* several years later, he said, "If they had punted, we would have been deep in our own territory. But Plum had hit two passes to Jim Gibbons,

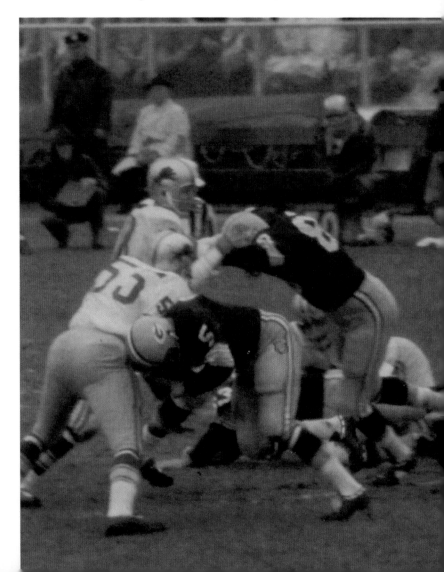

and he came back with the same play, only to Terry Barr. It might have worked, but Barr slipped on the wet field.

"When I picked the thing off, I could hear Vince Lombardi yelling, 'You got it, Herbie.' He always called me Herbie. Plum finally forced me out of bounds, and I could see he was really teed off. When I got up, I could hear people yelling outside the stadium as well as inside."

The ones outside missed Hornung and Taylor gaining five yards on a couple of running plays and Hornung kicking the winning field goal. But if they'd listened carefully, they might have heard the shouting in the Lions' locker room afterward.

It was reported that Karras threw his helmet at Plum and that Schmidt charged him. Brown couldn't recall either one of those things, but he said that didn't mean they didn't happen. It's not totally clear whether Wilson was just covering for his quarterback when he said he'd called the play, but that seems likely. There were no reports of anyone throwing anything at the coach.

Packers tight end Ron Kramer, who later played for the Lions, said he heard a lot of stories about that after he got to Detroit. "Yeah, I heard everything," he said. "Alex Karras was ready to kill Milton Plum. I don't know why he threw that pass."

Neither did Lombardi, but he politely declined to comment on the play afterwards. He would have plenty to say about the game, however, in a very popular book he did with W.C. Heinz that included a description of the week leading up to the game. The book was called *Run to Daylight*.

The Packers did just that many times after surviving that Sunday. The Lions still haven't.

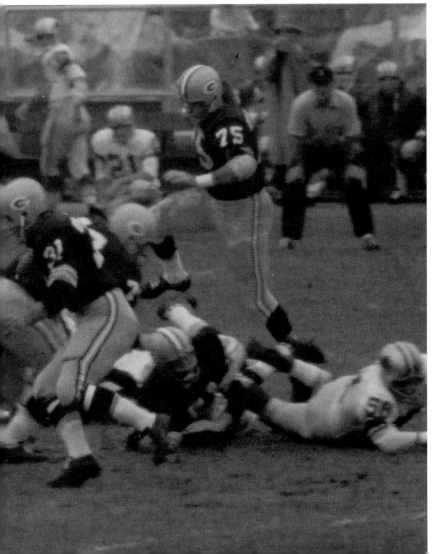

Jim Taylor (31), with a great lead block from Paul Hornung (5), finds a hole and makes the most of it. Taylor was the game's leading rusher with 95 yards on 20 carries.

Opposite page: Holder Joe
Theismann and kicker Mark
Moseley are a picture of dejection
after Moseley misses a 39-yard
field goal attempt with three seconds left in the highest scoring
game in Packers history.

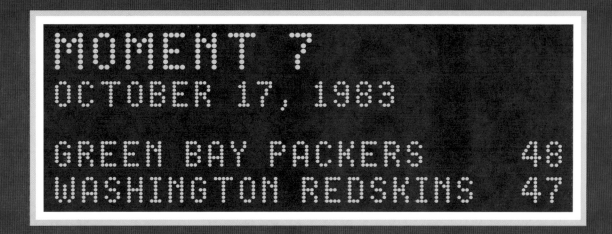

MOMENT 7
OCTOBER 17, 1983

GREEN BAY PACKERS   48
WASHINGTON REDSKINS   47

JUST PLAIN OFFENSIVE

Ironically, it began with a fumble. The world champion Washington Redskins had run for only a yard on their first two downs, and Joe Theismann decided it was time to do something different.

So he threw the ball, and the next thing he saw was linebacker Mike Douglass racing past him on a 22-yard dash to the goal line. Barely a minute had gone by and the first points were already on the board in the highest-scoring game in the Green Bay Packers' history.

Over the years, the Packers would put up more points in a game. In fact, they did it that same season. And they'd certainly give up more. The Bears had gouged them for 61 just three years earlier. But never in all their years in the league had they collaborated with anybody else on such a reckless display of offensive might.

Douglass remembers the first touchdown as if it were last week.

"It was a swing pass to Joe Washington," he said. "They ran the first two plays to our right side, and then on the third play they tried a screen to Washington. Right when he caught the ball and turned, I hit him and the ball came out. I picked it up, ran it into the end zone and spiked it. I was going, 'This is going to be a good night.'"

Douglass didn't know the half of it, but for none of the reasons he might have expected. From the moment the Packers' outside linebacker trotted back to the sideline until the final three seconds of the game when Washington's Mark Moseley pushed a 39-yard field goal attempt wide right, the contest was about anything but defense.

Washington's bobble was the only turnover the Packers forced all night. They gave up 552 yards, 33 first downs, five touchdowns and four field goals before the game ended 3 hours and 16 minutes after it started. They let their opponents score nine times in their 12 possessions and made them punt only once.

The Redskins also forced just one turnover. They allowed 473 yards, 23 first downs, six touchdowns and two field goals, and they let the Packers score 7 times in 10 possessions. Green Bay punted just twice, and the Redskins blocked one of them.

Monday Night Football viewers had never before seen so many points scored in one game. They still haven't. Neither has Green Bay.

The highest-scoring show in the Packers' history took place in the seventh game of the 1983 season. The second-highest? It occurred six

Lynn Dickey drops back behind Karl Swanke (67) and Dave Drechsler (61)

weeks later when the Packers lost, 47-41, in overtime at Atlanta. They also scored 55 points against Tampa Bay and 41 against Houston that year. Clearly these Packers were a one-trick pony. But it was a spellbinding trick.

Lynn Dickey had an unreasonably strong and accurate arm to go with three Pro Bowl receivers in James Lofton, John Jefferson and tight end Paul Coffman. They all caught more than 50 passes that year as did running back Gerry Ellis. The Packers averaged 27 points a start and went over 30 six times while gaining 386 yards a game. It was good enough to give them the league's second-leading offense, but it wasn't good enough to overcome the league's 28th-ranked defense.

Or to get into the post-season and save Bart Starr's job. Starr was fired after the team lost its last game in Chicago, finishing 8-8 and missing the playoffs for the eighth time in his nine-year reign. It was the last thing he would have expected after this dramatic victory.

Starr was keeping a secret as he prepared his 3-3 team to face a Washington powerhouse that would finish 14-2 and play in the Super Bowl for a second straight year. The secret involved his offensive line. Right guard Leotis Harris had gone down with a season-ending knee injury the week before, and backup Tim Huffman had a bad ankle, leaving the Packers dangerously vulnerable against Dave Butz, Washington's immense defensive tackle.

Starr's solution was to move right tackle Greg Koch to guard, but he didn't want to tip off the Redskins and give Butz a chance to study film on Koch. So he denied all week that Koch was working out at a new position. Veteran Charlie Getty started in Koch's tackle spot, and undersized Karl Swanke drew the assignment on Washington's Dexter Manley. It all worked beautifully as the retooled offensive line gave Dickey enough time to complete 22 passes in 31 attempts for 387 yards.

"We didn't really have a guard who matched up with Butz very well, and I was pretty much the strongest guy on the team," Koch said. "He was 6-7 and about 325. They listed me at 276, but I was about 295. He was just a big guy and hard to maneuver around, but he didn't give you any fancy pass rush moves, so he was a perfect guy for me. If you want to put strength on strength, it was good for me."

Washington's John Riggins works hard on one of his 25 carries for 98 yards.

While the Packers were keeping their plans to themselves, at least one Redskins player was going public, and Starr used his words as a rallying cry.

"They had a tight end from UCLA who made a comment to the media in Washington that he thought this game was going to be a rout," Dickey said. "Bart started off our Wednesday meeting with that quote. He put it up on the overhead view, so the whole team could see it. He said, 'That's what these guys think of you.'

"I think sometimes when you get bulletin board fodder, it kind of goes in one ear and out the other, but Bart thought it was really significant, and he was hanging on to that comment. As we were getting ready to come out for the introductions on game night, he put it back up on the overhead view and said, 'I know I've shown you guys this all week, but this guy said the game is going to be a rout, but what he didn't say was which way. Let's go out there and kick their ass.' We hadn't heard that from Bart before, and as an older player, that kind of got my attention."

Douglass got everyone's attention a few minutes later when he collided with Washington and opened the scoring. Redskins coach Joe Gibbs claimed that Washington never had possession of the ball, and the play should have been ruled an incomplete pass. But those were the days before instant replay, and this would not be a game decided by officials. Only six penalties were called all night, three on each team.

Theismann got the touchdown back by taking the Redskins on a 6-play, 55-yard drive, giving the Packers a preview of his performance by hitting on passes of 34

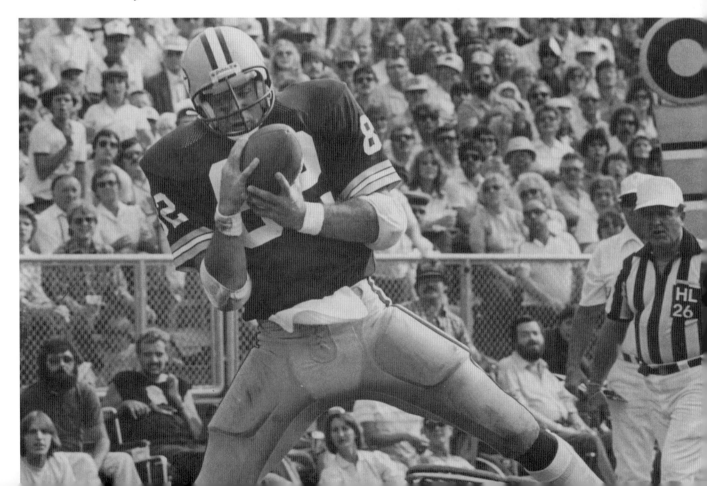

Tight end Paul Coffman was a popular target for Lynn Dickey. He had six catches against the Redskins for 124 yards.

Theismann has plenty of time to get off this pass, one of 39 he threw against the Packers.

and 14 yards along the way. He would complete 27 of 39 for 398 yards, although the Redskins were trying to balance their offense while the Packers had a one-track mind. They ran the ball only 18 times to Washington's 43 and gained just 70 yards on the ground to the Skins' 184. And that resulted in the oddest statistic of all: time of possession.

Washington held the ball 39 minutes and 5 seconds, while the Packers had it only 20 minutes and 55 seconds and never for more than 4 minutes on any scoring drive. They brought new meaning to the term "quality time," averaging more than two points a minute.

"We started out the season gangbusters (beating Houston 41-38)," said center Larry McCarren, "but the coaches kind of thought, 'We can't get in games like this because we're going to get outscored.' So they tried to make it a little more of a ball control offense, and it didn't work. It wasn't our personnel or personality, and we struggled a little bit trying to do that.

"Before the Monday night game, Bill Meyers, who was the assistant offensive line coach at the time, came up while we were stretching and said, 'Don't worry about it tonight. Sneaky says the defense is going to have to take care of itself, we're going for it.' And that's what we did. We ran every crazy play that we had, and they all worked." "Sneaky" was Bob Schnelker, the Packers' offensive coordinator, and he would be given the game ball that night, his 55th birthday.

"We ran the ball just enough to keep them off-balance," Dickey said. "I think Bob felt all along that if we got time we could chew them up. They weren't getting a good pass rush at all. Unfortunately for Greg, he had to be over Dave Butz, and Butz was head-butting him all the time. I remember Greg would come back in the huddle and say, 'That big ox is pounding on me.' But Greg could do anything. He was really tough and really smart. There was no one in the league who scared Greg Koch.

"Karl Swanke had Dexter Manley, and he actually got in a fight with him early in the game. I'd never seen Karl Swanke fight with anybody, but he had that little spunk in him that night, and he took care of Manley the whole game."

Dickey meanwhile was taking maximum advantage of the time provided by his line. He'd been feeling great before the game, and things just kept getting better the longer he played. "In warm-ups I made the comment to Paul Coffman that 'I don't know if I could throw a wobbly pass tonight if I tried,'" he said. "I never threw a real wobbly pass anyway, but some days it would just come out better than others."

It came out particularly well for Coffman, who led Green Bay's receivers with 6 catches for 124 yards. "Dickey was on fire, and they benched Curtis Jordan because he couldn't cover Paul," Koch said. "I knew Curtis from Texas Tech. It was kind of embarrassing for him."

But the Packers patched-up defense was having its own problems, and they started up front. Defensive end Mike Butler, whom the Packers had taken ninth overall in the 1977 draft, had left in July for Tampa Bay of the United States Football League. Terry Jones, an underrated nose tackle, tore his Achilles tendon in the first game of the season, and Rich Turner, his replacement, was lost five weeks later with a knee injury.

That left Charlie Johnson as the starting nose tackle and Daryle Skaugstad as his understudy-a castoff backed up by a reject. Starr had also cut starting free safety Maurice Harvey and defensive end Casey Merrill after the season started, leaving defensive coordinator John Meyer's group in disarray. And it showed as the two offenses landed one haymaker after another.

With 2:50 to play the Redskins went up, 47-45, on Theismann's 3-yard touchdown pass to Washington, and three plays later the Packers appeared to be on their death bed facing a third and ten from their own 36-yard line. But Ellis revived them by combining with Dickey on a 56-yard pass play that carried them to the Washington 8. It might have carried to the end zone if anyone else but Darrell Green had been chasing him.

"I faked the guy outside and came back inside, and the ball was already coming," Ellis said. "I caught it with one arm, and I was going down the field thinking, 'I've got this touchdown.' Then I happened to look over my shoulder, and the fastest guy in football was there. He caught me on the 8, and that actually might have been a good thing for us because it allowed us to run some time off the clock."

Green Bay ate up some time by running the ball three more times before Jan Stenerud nailed a 20-yard field goal with 54 seconds to play. Those would be the last points of the game, although it certainly didn't look like it at the time. Incredibly the Redskins were able to take the kickoff and march 51 yards in 46 seconds while the Packers' prevent defense sat back and admired their work.

"When they started that drive, they had no timeouts,

and they just went down the field," Dickey said. "Unbelievable. I remember Joe Washington would come out of the backfield and catch not 5-yard outs but 12-yard outs. And there was no one there. I mean no one. You'd think you'd funnel everything inside, put people along the sideline, and if they get in the middle of the field, you tackle them and eat up a lot of time.

"I remember telling one of the coaches on defense, 'You've got to move the guys up. Funnel them inside.' He looked at me and went, 'Yeah, yeah, you're probably right.' I thought, 'Oh man.' Our guys were 15 yards downfield. It didn't make any sense. John Anderson could run. Mad Dog (Douglass) could run. They were just doing what they were told."

Douglass couldn't agree more. "It was poorly called," he said. "It was like the coaches panicked."

The whole stadium was near panic when Theismann completed an 18-yard pass to Charlie Brown, setting up Moseley's 39-yard attempt with 3 seconds to play. Moseley, a 12-year veteran, had been named the NFL's Most Valuable Player the year before when he'd made 20 field goals in 21 tries. He already had 12 game-winning kicks on his resume, and he'd have two more before the season was over.

He'd been perfect from 42, 28, 31 and 28 yards so far that night, and there wasn't much reason to think he wouldn't stay that way. "James Lofton and I were sitting there going, 'Oh well,'" Ellis said, "and the next thing I know the crowd erupts. The best kicker in the league blew a chip shot. That's what won the game for us."

That and the 473 yards total offense and the eight scores.

"It was a tennis match," Koch said. "The thing I'll never forget is John Meyer saying after the game was over, 'It may not seem like it, but I thought we played pretty well defensively.' And I thought, 'If what's-his-name makes that kick, they beat us 50-48.' I thought that was a pretty funny statement. I thought John was a good coach, but it just struck me as funny."

Ninety-five points and 1,025 yards after Mike Douglass picked up a loose ball, somebody had to come away smiling.

Jan Stenerud kicks the winning field goal in the highest-scoring Monday night game ever.

Opposite page: Under pressure in more ways than one, Zeke Bratkowski has a huge playoff game against the Baltimore Colts and Tom Matte.

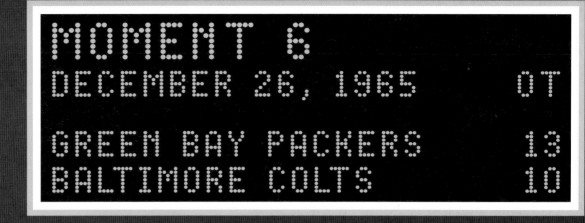

MOMENT 6

DECEMBER 26, 1965   OT

GREEN BAY PACKERS   13
BALTIMORE COLTS   10

SOMETHING TO KICK ABOUT

It was only fair. The Baltimore Colts came to Lambeau Field without Johnny Unitas, and one play into the 1965 Western Conference playoff game, the Packers were without Bart Starr.

While one Hall of Fame quarterback could only watch, the other completed his only pass of the day to tight end Billy Anderson, who promptly fumbled the ball. It was picked up by Baltimore's Don Shinnick, turning Starr into a defender. Starr knew he couldn't stop Shinnick from getting into the end zone, but he thought if he could strip away a blocker, maybe somebody else could. Wrong decision.

The Colts' Jim Welch buried Starr, Shinnick scored, and Starr had to be helped from the field with badly bruised ribs. He never got back into the game except to hold for place-kicks.

And so began one of the most bizarre and hotly contested victories in the Packers' playoff history. It was a game that started with injured quarterbacks and should have ended with an errant kick. Or so the Colts insisted.

Chandler's 25-yard field goal 13 minutes and 39 seconds into sudden death sent 50,484 fans home happy that Sunday, but it was a different Chandler kick that convinced the visitors that the wrong team had advanced to the NFL championship game with Cleveland.

That one came from the Baltimore 22 with 1:58 to play in regulation, and it tied the score at 10. The officials said it was three points, but the Colts said it was wide right by three feet. They're still saying it.

"I couldn't believe they called it good," Colts defensive tackle Fred Miller said, no less adamant 40-plus years later. "It was obvious. The place I was standing was pretty much in a direct line with the goal posts. We had a couple of players on the field when the game was over, me being one of them, who would probably have taken a swing at the official if he had been on the field. Fortunately, they had skedaddled.

"After you rushed, you turned around and looked. Just about everybody turned around and looked. Chandler was looking. He ducked his head because he knew it was bad. Go back and look at the game films. When he kicked the field goal, you'll see him turn in disgust."

Miller doesn't get much of an argument from Chandler, who says he really can't say for sure if the kick was good. Instead, he defers to Starr, who was the holder on the play.

"Ask Bart Starr," he said. "I didn't think it was,

Bart Starr is down and out of the game after suffering a rib injury on the first play from scrimmage.

but I didn't see it until it was beyond the uprights. He said it went through and curved out. That's all I can say. I threw my head up like I had missed it, but then again, I didn't see it until it was beyond the uprights. It was very short. I didn't hit it like I'd like, but hey, they counted it. That's all that counts."

Starr is much more positive when he's asked if he thought the kick was good. "I didn't think," he said. "It was good. I'm sitting on the field or standing on the field looking at it. It was in."

Sitting or standing was about all Starr could do at the time as Zeke Bratkowski took over for him. He was able to come in for the hold, although he could only get his arms to about chest level.

"If he had snapped me a high one, I would have been in trouble," Starr said. "I believe I tore something, so I had to come out. I tried to throw some balls on the sidelines, but I couldn't throw the ball. Typically, Zeke did a hell of a job."

Good enough to get the Packers into only the second overtime in NFL history. The first was the 1958 championship match between Baltimore and the New York Giants, which is frequently dubbed "The Greatest Game Ever Played." While this one wasn't as great as that one, it was almost as memorable because of the man who played quarterback for the losing team. This was the famous Tom Matte game.

Matte was a Colts running back who hadn't played quarterback since he'd left Ohio State where Woody Hayes treated

Running back Tom Matte (41) is pressed into service as a starting quarterback, and he needs help from a wristband that contains the Colts' plays.

FR-OLFR	FRS-OLFRS	WL.	DWR	OLDWRS	SHOT RT
ROLL LEFT	39 SP.	3TT	19 ST	ROLL LEFT	QB 15G
19U	39 SW.	15G	15G	29 ST	" 14G
17P	35 Su.	P1UBacker	52	25+C	" 34T
25LAG*	35 SP	24LAG	P16+C	15G	" 33T
5 EYE	35T	14 EYE	14G	QB 52	QB. S3
15G	25+C	14G	18 ST	52	38 Sweep
P10+C	QB52	16P	18 C.B.	C34 ST	QB.43B
1B 34T	D31+33T			C 334 ST	260 Dog
14G	QB STATUE RIGHT (OVER)	ROLL RT	76 OH	266 CHERRY T.O	362 Deep M
36T		16U	76 T.O.		
18CB			76 D.Q	66 ARROW	7RS
PASS	60 ALL HOOK BASIC REX LEX	ROLL RT	76 Quick	66 Diag.	34 Special 35"
ROLL LEFT		24LAC PASS		SHORT YD:	32T
25LAG			SCREEN TO LENNY	7R	Sneak 25U
5607B DELAY	260 DOG HOOK CHERRY T.O LEX			P-10	WR
68 BASIC CIRCLE				36T	P10
266 CHERRY T.O.				R14 Keep	33T
				ROLL LEFT	16P 31T Roll RT

the forward pass as a last resort. And Matte wouldn't have played quarterback this time if the Colts hadn't been slammed by a perfect storm of injuries and rejections on the league level.

Unitas, the league's reigning Most Valuable Player, went down in the 12th game of 1965 while Baltimore was being shut out by the Chicago Bears. He underwent knee surgery immediately following the December 5 game, and he was replaced by third-year pro Gary Cuozzo. But not for long. Cuozzo separated his left shoulder the following weekend in a doubly devastating 42-27 loss to the Packers in Baltimore that not only cost the Colts their second-string quarterback but the lead in the Western Conference.

After Cuozzo departed for surgery, Baltimore activated 20th-round draft choice George Haffner and claimed veteran Ed Brown from Pittsburgh on waivers for the final game of the regular season against the Los Angeles Rams. Matte started, but it was Brown who helped beat the Rams with a 68-yard touchdown pass. Meanwhile the Packers were getting tied by San Francisco.

That left both teams at 10-3-1, but two things were working against the Colts for the conference playoff game. They had lost a December 6 coin flip to determine where the game would be played if there was a tie at the top of the standings. And the NFL had declined owner Carroll Rosenbloom's request for an exception to the rule requiring a player to be on the roster for at least two games to be eligible for the playoffs. That disqualified Haffner and Brown and made Matte their quarterback.

The fifth-year former Buckeye threw only twice against the Rams in the regular season finale, reading the plays off a plastic coated wrist band that he called a "peep sheet." He took that sheet with him to

Green Bay where the Packers dared him to put the ball in the air.

"We scouted Matte when he played the game before ours, and we saw that his passing was suspect," recalled linebacker Dave Robinson. "We decided we were going to play what amounted to a goal line defense the whole game where we hit the gaps and strictly played the run. What hurt us in that game was that Bart got hurt, and our offense suffered. Everybody says 'Tom Matte, Tom Matte.' Hell, we won that game with our second quarterback, too."

The difference was the Packers' second choice was a quarterback by trade. Matte finished the game completing five out of 12 passes for 40 yards, while Bratkowski hit on 22 of 39 for 248 yards. But Bratkowski also threw two interceptions as the Packers committed four turnovers to Baltimore's one, keeping the Colts alive even though they were outgained, 362 yards to 175.

With a running back at quarterback, the Colts were still able to take a 10-0 halftime lead. Meanwhile, the problems were outnumbering the solutions for the Packers offense. They needed a bad snap on a Baltimore punt to get on the board in the third quarter. Paul Hornung scored on a one-yard run, but then he missed the overtime with an assortment of injuries. So did wide-out Boyd Dowler, and for a while it looked as if

Opposite page: Paul Hornung (5) is escorted by Jerry Kramer on a sweep.

Don Chandler kicks the sudden death field goal that gives the Packers the Western Conference championship. Though Starr's injured ribs didn't allow him to pass, he was able to hold for both of Chandler's field goals.

Bratkowski might be gone, too, when the Colts' Miller leveled him late in the game. Third-stringer Dennis Claridge was warming up when Bratkowski decided he could go on.

A hotly contested facemask call kept the Packers' game-tying drive alive in the fourth quarter until they arrived on the Baltimore 15 with just over 2 minutes left in regulation. That put Chandler in the spotlight, which was an unlikely place for him.

Vince Lombardi had picked up Chandler from the New York Giants for a third-round draft choice during the off-season. Chandler had made only 9 of 20 field goal attempts for the Giants in 1964, but Lombardi reasoned that that was better than the 12 of 38 that Hornung had made for the Packers. And Chandler did turn out to be a steady presence for the Packers for three championship seasons

He wasn't so steady this time, though. With the goal posts on the goal line, the tying 22-yarder didn't appear to be a terribly demanding kick, but the Colts insisted he missed it anyway. "If that kick was good, I'll eat the football," Miller said after the game.

Judging from his body language, Chandler agreed. Lombardi even barked at him when he ran off the field after hanging his head. "He told me not to do that anymore," Chandler said.

Fortunately for the Packers, the situation did not come up again. Chandler's next attempt in overtime left no doubt. The Colts had the first chance to win the game in the extra period, but after Lou Michaels' 47-yard field goal attempt was short, Bratkowski led the Packers on a drive that left Chandler with a 25-yard attempt.

"It went right down the middle," Chandler said. "There wasn't any question about that. But I was shaking like a leaf after the game. I don't think people understand the pressure involved in that."

While Chandler shook, the Colts stewed, and they still hadn't given up the argument almost a year later. The following November, ABC-TV released a film that the network claimed proved that the tying field goal was wide. If that was true, it was a mistake the league tried to avoid making again when it extended the uprights to 20 feet above the crossbar and painted them bright yellow in time for the 1966 season.

But first the Packers had to deal with the Browns in the NFL championship game at Lambeau Field the next week. Chandler kicked three field goals as they beat Cleveland, 23-12. None of them was disputed.

Opposite page: Vince Lombardi shares a happy post-game moment with Zeke Bratkowski, who completed 22 of 39 passes for 248 yards as Starr's replacement.

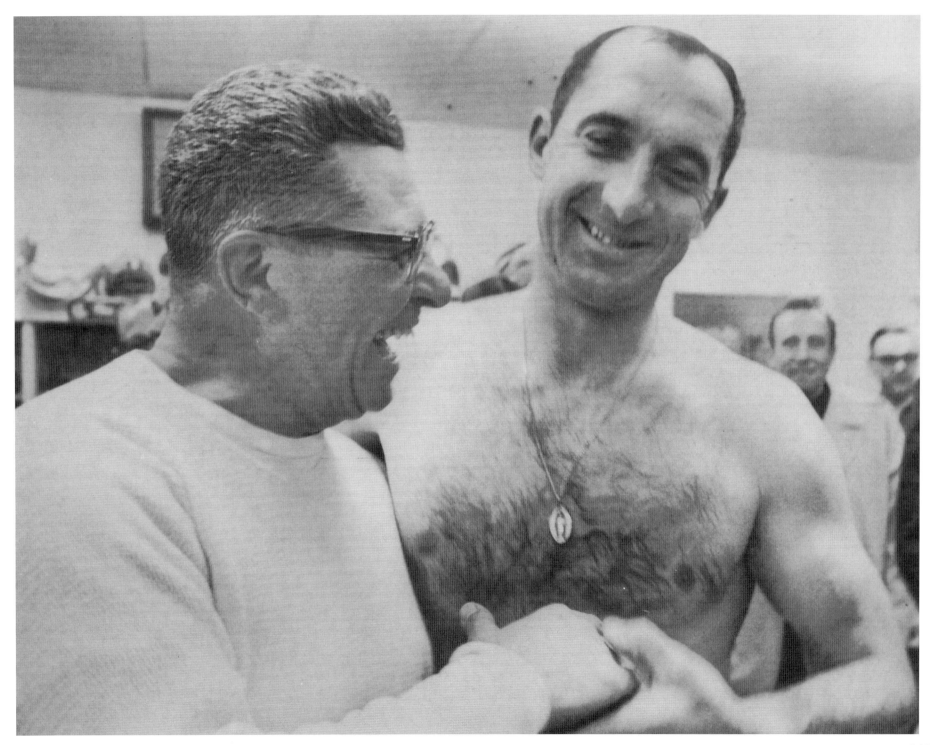

141

Opposite page: Vice President
Richard Nixon shares the podium with
(from left) Miss America Marilyn
Elaine Van Derbur, former coach Gene
Ronzani, NFL Commissioner Bert Bell,
Gov. Vernon Thomson, Congressman
John Byrnes and Chicago Bears
President George Halas in the first
game at Lambeau Field.

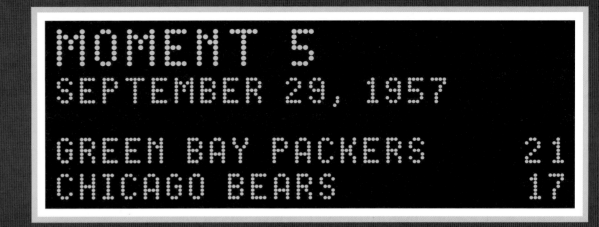

MOMENT 5
SEPTEMBER 29, 1957

GREEN BAY PACKERS   21
CHICAGO BEARS   17

NOW *THAT'S* DEDICATION

The Packers stifled the Chicago Bears' offense in the second half of the first game ever played at Lambeau Field, proving beyond all doubt that you can never have too many Dillons at a dedication.

Safety Bobby Dillon upstaged Marshall Matt Dillon when he intercepted an Ed Brown pass with 3:59 to play, locking up a victory that Green Bay absolutely had to have. Losing to the Bears at home is always unthinkable for the Packers, and losing to them in their brand new $960,000 stadium would have been unspeakable.

Five interceptions, including another one by Dillon, and a fourth quarter touchdown pass by Vito "Babe" Parilli avoided that catastrophe and capped a weekend that might be described as a great party interrupted by a good football game.

Lambeau Field wouldn't become Lambeau Field for another eight years when it was renamed at an exhibition game, but the actual concrete and steel structure opened for business on a pretty September Sunday, and the city made quite a fuss over it. Honored guests included Vice President Richard Nixon and actor James Arness, a.k.a. Marshall Matt Dillon, who at the time was the country's favorite TV cowboy. Miss America was there, too, as were Miss Wisconsin and Miss Wisconsin Universe.

It all might have gone up in Gunsmoke, though, if Parilli hadn't thrown a 6-yard touchdown pass to Gary Knafelc with 8:21 remaining in this monumental upset of the defending Western Conference champions. The victory turned out to be one of the rare things that went right in a 3-9 season under Lisle Blackbourn that would be followed by a 1-10-1 season under Scooter McLean.

About the only thing worse than the Packers teams in those days were the Packers' facilities, and so when the citizens of Green Bay passed a referendum to replace old City Stadium with new City Stadium, the players were beyond grateful.

Knafelc remembers it well. "It was like you had died and gone to heaven," he said. "Our locker rooms were under the bleachers in the old place, and they had mesh lockers. The equipment room had a dirt floor enclosed with mesh. The first time I went there I was told to pick out some shoulder pads. There were three or four pairs of shoulder pads that were like grade school stuff lying on the floor, and so I called my father and had him send me the shoulder pads I wore in the all-star game. I wore those for three years. We had nothing."

What they had was a 25,000-seat wooden antique owned and operated by the school board and shared with East High School since 1925, and that was an improvement over their previous homes. Earlier, they'd occupied Hagemeister Park and then Bellevue Park, which was basically a baseball field.

What they got was the first stadium in America built exclusively for pro football, thanks to local taxpayers who, after years of talking about it, passed a referendum in April of 1956. Construction began early the next year, and people started filing into the place less than 18 months after the referendum passed. These were different times.

The stadium was placed on open land at the edge of town, and it was anything but fancy by today's standards.

Actor James Arness, a.k.a. Marshall Matt Dillon, leaves the Northland Hotel in downtown Green Bay.

It was surrounded by a cyclone fence, and the upper stands behind the end zones that would later make it a bowl weren't part of the original plan. There was a small locker room at the south end, but not enough room for the Packers' offices, which remained downtown.

The referendum got a boost from Bears owner George Halas of all people, who spoke at a downtown pep rally four days before the vote. According to the *Green Bay Press-Gazette*, Halas told the 1,000 or so in attendance, "I can say to you sincerely — just as sincerely as we hope to edge out the Packers in both games next fall — that the best way for you to guarantee the current and future success of the Packers is to build the new stadium."

It may have come as a shock to the audience that Halas cared at all about the current and future success of the Packers, but Papa Bear had a point. Without a decent place to play, the franchise might not have stayed afloat, and the NFL would have missed it. Speaking at the opening game, NFL Commissioner Bert Bell gushed, "The dedication of this stadium today is the greatest thing that has ever happened in professional football."

Since Bell had been around the league for 24 years, that was a mouthful, but he wasn't any more enthusiastic about the place than the Packer players. Parilli still remembers how he felt moving in.

Babe Parilli led the Packers to victory after coming on in relief of Bart Starr.

"It was like the Taj Mahal compared to East High," he said. "Back then, you had to appreciate those things. Now you've got so much. It's so overwhelming, and you take it for granted. But we were pretty overwhelmed then. I was anyway."

And so was the city. A parade was held on Saturday, and police estimated that 70,000 people lined the 2 ½ mile route. Another 18,000 showed up at old City Stadium where Marshall Dillon arrived in a convertible and was surrounded by a tidal wave of kids whom the cops couldn't seem to keep off the field.

The TV lawman distributed autographed pictures, and his co-star at the event played "Tenderly" and "Tea for Two" on the organ, according to the *Press-Gazette*. Her name was Marilyn Elaine Van Derbur of Denver, Colorado, and she had just been elected Miss America. Also on the program were baton twirlers, clowns, a western music combo, a drill team and a corps of former Packer players dating all the way back to 1919. The Green Bay Premontre High School band wrapped up the festivities by playing "Taps" for the old stadium, a number that may have resonated with Miss America, whose father owned a string of mortuaries.

The dedication ceremonies the next day were no less elaborate. Curly Lambeau sent a telegram, and Nixon congratulated the 32,132 customers and their fellow citi-

zens for building the place without asking Washington for money. The vice president also predicted that the Packers would win championships there, and the Milwaukee Braves would win the 1957 World Series. He was right both ways.

Meanwhile, everyone was trying to get close to Ms Van Derbur, and fullback Fred Cone recalls an interesting story about that. "Jim Ringo was posing with Miss America down on the sidelines," he said, "and he put his arm around her waist and let his hand slip down a little bit. I think she almost slapped him. She wasn't having any part of that."

Fortunately, nobody got hurt at halftime, and the field was cleared so that the football game could continue. The Packers had come back from 7-0 and 14-7 deficits to tie the score at intermission, getting their touchdowns on a 38-yard pass from Parilli to Billy Howton and a one-yard run by Cone. But George Blanda's 13-yard field goal put the Bears back up again in the third quarter and made it possible for Parilli and Knafelc to become heroes.

Ironically, Parilli wouldn't even have been in the game if Bart Starr had had a better day. Starr started, but Blackbourn replaced him with Parilli in the second quarter, establishing a pattern for the two to share the job for the next two seasons. The Packers had created a vacancy at the position by sending Tobin Rote to Detroit in a six-player deal two days before training

Upper: Fans say good-bye to old City Stadium on the Saturday before the game.

Lower: Lambeau Field starts from the ground up.

146

DEDICATION PROGRAM

GREEN BAY
PACKERS
VS
CHICAGO
BEARS

SUNDAY 1:05 P.M.

SEPTEMBER 29, 1957

PRICE 50c

I'M A PACKER BACKER
STADIUM Dedication SEPT. 29-51

Left: The official program of the first game played at Lambeau, then City Stadium.

Above: The official pin from "Dedication Day."

camp, and Blackbourn never could make up his mind on a starter.

"We were always having problems," Knafelc said. "When Rote left, it was up in the air. Bart was very consistent. Babe was a little more flamboyant. He could run around, scramble and that kind of thing. They were two entirely different types of quarterbacks. Parilli was a little more athletic."

Which on this occasion was a good thing because the Bears had flushed him out of the pocket on the play that won the game for the Packers, and he had to buy time before he found Knafelc in the end zone.

"Babe was running for his life on the far left side, and he just threw the ball into the end zone," Knafelc said. "I was on the left side and came across. He saw me over there, and we always had a deal with Babe. We yelled, 'Vito, Vito, Vito.' I was kind of in a slot. I had run a post pattern, but he was running so hard to his left that I had to come back to the left side and find an open spot. That's where he saw me, and he threw the ball behind me."

Not so far behind that Knafelc couldn't catch it, though. The extra point put the Packers up by four points, and their defense stymied the Bears for the last 8½ minutes with the help of Dillon's interception and a fumbled punt by Chicago. The fans went crazy, and the players were pretty happy, too.

"I guess we had a little more adrenalin going that day because of the big crowd," Cone said.

Maybe Marshall Dillon and Miss America helped, too. It would be 13 months before the Packers won another home game.

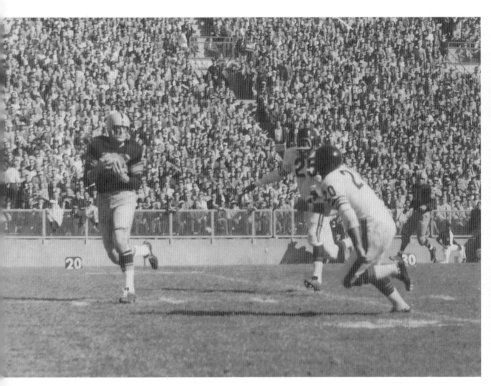 

Left: Bill Howton scores the Packers' first touchdown on a 38-yard pass from Babe Parilli.

Right: The Packers cheerleaders perform during the halftime festivities.

Opposite Page: Gary Knafelc, between the goal posts, hits the turf after catching the winning touchdown pass.

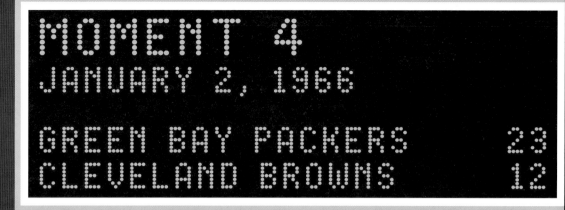

MOMENT 4
JANUARY 2, 1966

GREEN BAY PACKERS   23
CLEVELAND BROWNS   12

NEVER TOO OLD

It took an hour and 20 minutes for the team bus to make it from the Cleveland Browns' hotel in Appleton to Lambeau Field, normally more than enough time for a round trip. But there would be nothing normal about this day for the defending NFL champions.

Not only would they arrive at the stadium late, but their offense would leave it early, their passing game in tatters, their running game abandoned and their crown back on the Packers' heads.

The Browns had an 11-3 record, an MVP at fullback and a Ph.D. at quarterback. The Packers had a 10-3-1 record and a pair of running backs who were aging, infirm and incredibly willing. Their names were Paul Hornung and Jim Taylor, and both of them would be gone in a couple of years.

So would Cleveland's Jim Brown, the league's Most Valuable Player and eight-time rushing leader. This would be Brown's last game, although no one knew it at the time. He walked away from football after nine full seasons, but the Packers made him disappear one game sooner than he'd planned by holding him to 50 yards rushing.

That number as much as anything explained the Browns' futility, although the weather did play a part. Four inches of snow fell in Green Bay on this 33-degree Sunday, and it rained and sleeted, too. Sometimes all in the same hour. By the time the game was over, the field lights were on, and the Browns wouldn't have been surprised to see a volcano erupting at the 50-yard line.

But that was hardly an excuse. These guys were from Cleveland after all, a place that nobody has ever confused with Aruba. The Browns could have overcome the elements, but they had no chance to overcome the Packers after the first half.

Coaches love total team efforts, and this victory was a textbook case of that for the Packers. Their defense produced two interceptions and held the Browns to 161 total yards or less than half of Green Bay's output. Their special teams blocked a Lou Groza field goal attempt and hurried the Browns into a missed extra point. Their offensive line opened the kind of lanes that the Browns' bus driver could only dream about on his way over from the Holiday Inn, and it protected Bart Starr as if he were an endangered species. In a way he was.

A case of badly bruised ribs suffered a week before in the Western Conference playoff game left Starr unsure of whether he even could throw until the Thursday before the game. But

Trying to warm up is a major challenge for both teams on snow-covered Lambeau Field.

he completed 10 of 18 passes for 147 yards and a touchdown anyway.

And then he and 50,777 soaked ticket holders settled back and watched Taylor and Hornung peel away the years and do their work. Hornung would carry the ball 18 times and gain 105 yards. Taylor would take it 27 times and pick up 96 yards and the keys to a new automobile. He got the car by being named the game's Most Valuable Player, although he could easily have shared it with Hornung.

How ironic that a pair of veterans who seemed so ready to hit the road should drive away from this championship game in such style. During the regular season, they had both turned 30, a veritable mid-life crisis for NFL running backs, and they could both see their replacements standing in the wings. The Packers had recently signed first-round draft choices Jim Grabowski and Donny Anderson to contracts totaling an unheard of $1.05 million, and the young pair was clearly the future of the Packer backfield.

Taylor had run for 734 yards during the regular season, missing 1,000 for the first time since 1959, and Hornung had managed only 299 yards on 89 carries. Taylor was struggling with a groin injury, and Hornung hurt everywhere. Knee, ribs, wrist, shoulder--they were all out of whack. No wonder the Packers finished 10th among 14 NFL teams in rushing while the Browns finished first. But Vince Lombardi understood that there was still some giddy-up in his two warhorses, and he used everything he could to spur them.

"Before the game, coach Lombardi called me in to his office and said, 'I don't know if you know this or not, but Jim Brown has never outgained Jim Taylor in a head-to-head match,'" recalled linebacker Dave Robinson. "I said, 'Really?' and he said, 'Yeah. You've got to help us make sure he doesn't do it this week.' I walked into the locker room later, and Lee Roy Caffey was sitting there, and he said, 'Dave, did Vince talk to you?' I said yes, and I told him what he'd said. He'd told Lee Roy the same thing. I told Lee Roy I didn't know what to say. Lee Roy said he told him to talk to Jim Taylor."

Lombardi's statistic was useful, even though it happened not to be true. Brown had outgained Taylor, 74 yards to 63, in a 1964 regular season game that the Packers won, 28-21. Taylor would remember that game well. He remembered every meeting with Cleveland and Brown.

"Jim always had a great game when Jimmy Brown was on the other side of the field because it was

Bart Starr is well protected by Bob Skoronski, Jim Taylor and Ken Bowman as he lets go of a first quarter pass.

Jimmy Brown," said guard Jerry Kramer. "He always wanted to be compared favorably to Jimmy Brown because Brown was the standard. And whenever we played Cleveland, we wanted Taylor to get more yards than Brown. So there was that factor."

Of course Kramer and his offensive friends could only affect half of the Taylor-Brown equation. The other half was up to the defense, which was fully aware that Brown carried the ball on 75% of Cleveland's running plays. The goal was always to contain him, and the Packers had just the man for the job in middle linebacker Ray Nitschke. Among Nitschke's most able assistants on this occasion was Willie Davis, the defensive end on the Browns' strong side.

"I have great respect for Jim Taylor, but Jim Brown was all-around the greatest running back ever to play the game," Robinson said. "If you didn't make adjustments for him, you were going to get your head handed to you. Nitschke keyed on him the whole game. Run or pass, Brown was the key. Ray thrived against the run. He loved to play the run and fire everybody else up, too. Once he got a hit, the adrenalin would start running, and he'd start talking, and when he started talking he picked everybody up.

"Willie always had great games against the Browns. He'd been traded by the Browns to the Packers, and it was like he was trying to prove they'd made a mistake. He just went down and got something extra. They had played him as an offensive tackle at Cleveland and then traded him to Green Bay when Paul Brown said, 'If you don't play for me, I'll trade you to Siberia.'"

Brown's version of Siberia was, of course, Green Bay, and on this day they were pretty much the same place, except that the traffic was lighter in Siberia. Freezing rain and snow-packed roads created massive jams that caused thousands to miss the kickoff. The tardy were in for a surprise when they turned on their car radios to catch the action because broadcasters Ted Moore and Blaine Walsh hadn't gotten there either until the Packers' fourth play from scrimmage.

Sixty grounds crew members and 25 volunteers shoveled three inches of snow off the tarp before it could be rolled up, and a couple of Jeeps were used to brush the white stuff off the playing surface. The Packers hired a helicopter to dry off the field and help clear the seating areas, but that didn't work, so the shovelers had to do the stands, too. Governor Warren Knowles had been planning to take in the event, but he went home after his plane circled Austin Straubel Field for a half-hour and couldn't land. It was not a great day for the aerial game.

At least not for the Browns' aerial game. Starr used his to put the Packers ahead, 7-0, on their first series of downs. He collaborated with Carroll Dale on a 47-yard touchdown pass and then admitted after the game that the ball had actually slipped out of his hand. But Dale had plenty of time to come back and get it.

Cleveland quarterback Frank Ryan held a doctorate degree in mathematics from Rice University, and he was smart enough to spot some holes in the Packer secondary on the Browns' first drive. He needed just three passes to cover 66 yards for a touchdown. Green Bay made all the necessary adjustments after that, and Ryan completed only five more passes for 48 yards the rest of the afternoon.

Ryan's scoring pass went 17 yards to Gary Collins at the expense of cornerback Herb Adderley, who learned that sometimes it doesn't pay to advertise.

"Herb hadn't had a touchdown pass thrown on him all year," Robinson said, "and before the game he was interviewed by a Cleveland newspaper or somebody, and they asked him how he was going to stop (Paul) Warfield and Collins. He said he studied the film, and he saw that Collins made a real gentle outside turn, and when he went to the post he never broke it off to the corner.

"The first time the Browns got down inside the 40, Collins hit it hard to the post, and when Herb closed on him Collins broke it to the corner for a touchdown. Vince used that I don't know how many times to teach us not to say a doggone word to the press."

Adderley's candor cost the Packers six points, but not the lead. That was preserved when Nitschke nailed Browns center John Morrow as he snapped the ball for Groza's extra point and sent it somewhere in the direction of Neenah. The kicker tried to pick up the ball and pass it, but that didn't work either.

Groza did manage a 24-yard field goal to give the Browns their only lead, but Don Chandler came back with two of those for the Packers from 15 and 23 yards. When Chandler was asked to recall what it was like kicking in Siberia, he replied, "Tolerable."

An adjective that could hardly be applied to the Cleveland offense after Groza's 28-yard field goal wrapped up the scoring for the visitors with 48 seconds and a whole second half to play.

Boyd Dowler (86) tries to elude Ross Fichtner (20) after hauling in a Starr pass.

Taylor plows through the mud for a small gain. He finished with 96 yards and was named Most Valuable Player of the 1965 NFL championship game.

156

The rest of the day belonged to the Packers' defense and of course their rushing game. Starr threw only five passes in the second half, completing four of them and leaving everything else up to Hornung and Taylor.

"Our running game made our passing game, so we felt going in that we could run the ball against them," Starr said. "And the conditions favored the run. Remember the '62 championship game against the Giants in New York? Windy and nasty. The Giants were a very good football team, but their running game wasn't very good, and you couldn't throw the ball because it was so damn windy. But we had the running game. I felt the same way about '65."

He felt it so strongly in fact that he handed the ball off nine times in the 11-play, 90-yard drive that accounted for the final 20-12 score a little more than halfway through the third quarter. To no one's surprise, Hornung got 42 of those yards, including the last 13 on a sweep.

"It was a championship game, and we always seemed to play better in big games," said Kramer. "Hornung was always that way. You could always count on him in a big ballgame."

Hornung appreciated the compliment, but then he'd heard it before from an unimpeachable source. "Lombardi always said, 'The bigger the game, the better Paul plays,'" Hornung said. "After a while you start believing that stuff."

He'd heard it said about Taylor as well, which seemed only natural to him.

"That's the way Lombardi's offense was," he said.

That notion was never truer than it was in this game, which served as kind of a last hurrah for the Packers' potent backfield tandem. Hornung and Taylor would both play one more season for Lombardi before the former retired and the latter moved on to New Orleans. Taylor led the Packers in rushing again in 1966 with 705 yards, but the injury-plagued Hornung gained only 200 yards and lost his starting job to Elijah Pitts.

Lombardi still had two championship seasons in him after the battle with the Browns, but he told everyone that this team had more character than any he'd ever been associated with.

He may have been right about that, and if he was, he had his running backs to thank on a snowy day at Lambeau Field when Jim Brown looked barely average.

Carroll Dale leaves Cleveland's Fichtner (20) and Walter Beach (49) in his wake as he hauls in a 47-yard touchdown pass on the first series of the game.

Opposite page: Brett Favre is interviewed by Terry Bradshaw as his
teammates look on following the
Packers 30-13 victory over the
Carolina Panthers in the 1996 NFC
championship game.

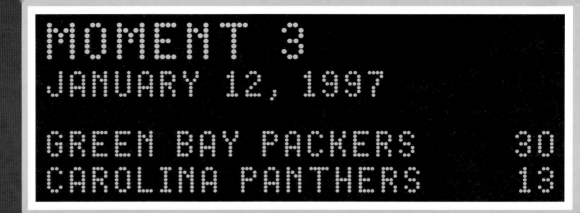

MOMENT 3
JANUARY 12, 1997

GREEN BAY PACKERS   30
CAROLINA PANTHERS   13

RETURN TO GLORY

The grass was from Maryland, the opponent was from North Carolina, and the weather was straight from the North Pole. Perfect conditions for earning a trip to the Super Bowl. And the Packers knew it, even when things started very badly.

On Green Bay's second possession of the NFC championship game, Brett Favre aimed a slant pass at Don Beebe, and Carolina linebacker Sam Mills jumped the route and took the interception 10 yards to the 2. Less than 10 minutes after the kickoff, the Panthers led, 7-0, but the home team never flinched.

The Packers had waited 29 years to get a chance at another NFL championship, and Carolina looked more like a minor inconvenience than a major obstacle. The expansion Panthers hadn't even been in the league three years earlier, while the Packers were in the playoffs for a fourth straight year.

Green Bay had finished first in the league in defense and fifth in offense while going 13-3 during the regular season. The 12-4 Panthers were tenth in defense and 23rd in offense, and their victory over Dallas in the divisional playoffs the previous week was considered an upset. The Packers were quarterbacked by Favre, who had just won his second straight Most Valuable Player award. Carolina was quarterbacked by Kerry Collins, who was adequate.

And of course the game was at Lambeau Field where the fans had never seen a playoff loss. The week before, the Packers had buried San Francisco, 35-14, during an all-day rain that had turned the field into a bog. New turf had been trucked in from a Maryland sod farm, and it held up beautifully, allowing the Packers to take maximum advantage of

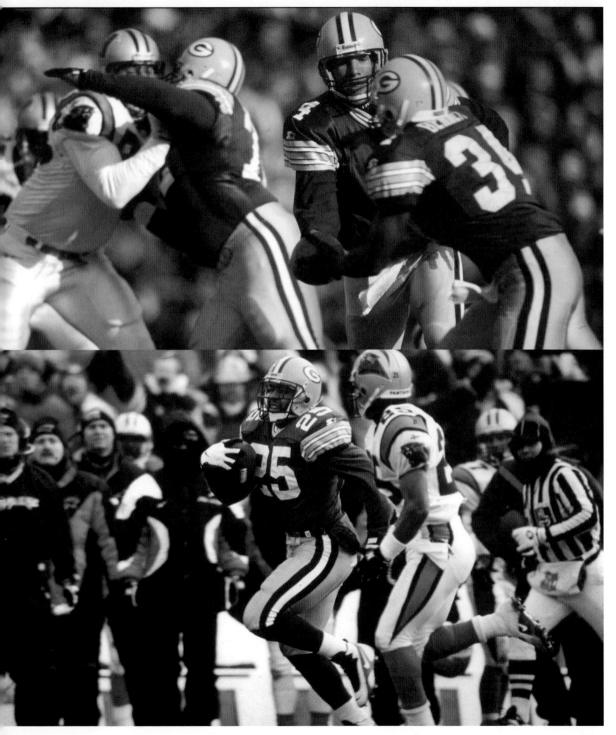

Favre's arm.

Now the sun was shining brightly, while the temperature was 3 degrees and the wind chill was minus-17. Green Bay couldn't have custom ordered a better day for facing a team from Dixie.

"It was the coldest game I'd played in," recalled defensive tackle Santana Dotson. "There was snow before the game, and they had concerns about it damaging the field. So they sent out a newsletter, and a lot of fans showed up to shovel off the field, which was a great thing in and of itself.

"When you're coming in from Tampa Bay or Carolina, you spend a lot of time looking at the Weather Channel trying to see exactly how cold it's going to be. But since you haven't practiced in it or lived in it, you can't really prepare for it. Then to come to play a talented team like we were in '96, it's really a lose-lose battle."

Except the Panthers didn't seem to understand that. Favre got that first touchdown back by throwing a 29-yard scoring pass to Dorsey Levens with six seconds gone in the second quarter. But then he fumbled when he was sacked on

Edgar Bennett (upper) and Dorsey Levens (lower) combined for 309 of the Packers' 479 total yards. Bennett rushed for 99 and Levens for 88, and they both scored touchdowns.

the Packers' next series, and Carolina got a 22-yard field goal from John Kasay. With 8:40 to go in the first half, the Panthers led, 10-7.

And then suddenly, the Packers seemed to remember who they were.

They allowed the Panthers to score only once more on a Kasay field goal in the third period while out-gaining them, 479 yards to 251 and out-rushing them, 201 yards to 45. The 479 total yards was a playoff record for Green Bay, and the 45 yards rushing was a franchise low for Carolina.

The Panthers' best chance to regain the momentum collapsed when Tyrone Williams intercepted a Collins pass with 42 seconds remaining in the second quarter. Four plays later, Chris Jacke kicked a 31-yard field goal, and the Packers took a 17-10 lead into halftime.

Just like that, Carolina's quick start was forgotten, and the rest of the afternoon served as preparation for the biggest celebration since the Ice Bowl.

"I just remember there was no panic," said tight end Mark Chmura. "It was almost as if we went into the game knowing we were going to win."

For at least one Packer there was no "almost."

"Carolina was an expansion team, and I knew they didn't have a chance," said safety LeRoy Butler. "We were such a good team. Even in the three games we lost, we just beat ourselves. The coaches were great, the players were great, and everybody loved one another.

"The atmosphere before the game was electric. The fans just kind of knew we were going to win. They were holding up signs saying what the score was going to be, and they actually had tears in their eyes when it was over because they were so happy that we'd made it to the Super

Reggie White celebrates with Brett Favre.

Bowl. We went into the game saying, 'We don't care who the hero is going to be, we've got to do everything possible to win this game for these fans.'"

There was certainly no shortage of heroes. Edgar Bennett ran for 99 yards, out-gaining the Carolina ground game all by himself, and he wasn't even the Packers' most effective back. That was Dorsey Levens, who totaled 205 yards on 88 rushing and 117 receiving. The Panthers, who prided themselves on having one of the league's top rushing defenses, couldn't believe anyone could mistreat them so badly on the ground. They simply never found an answer for the combination of Levens and Bennett and the blocking of fullback William Henderson.

Mike Holmgren congratulates the troops in a jubilant Green Bay locker room.

"That's when we started using the three-headed monster because we had to give everybody roles," said running backs coach Harry Sydney. "We talked as a staff, Mike Holmgren, (offensive coordinator) Sherman Lewis and myself and decided Dorsey was our single-back guy, Edgar was our two-back guy except in goal line, and Henderson was our hired hit man."

Sydney said the offensive line played incredibly, but then the Panthers' defense was constantly off balance because Favre was throwing so well that the Panthers never knew what to expect.

Favre passed for 292 yards and two touchdowns and directed scoring drives of 73, 71, 48, 73, 74 and 36 yards, and the kicking game wasn't bad either. Jacke booted three field goals, boosting his team record playoff total to 61 points.

The defense, meanwhile, produced three turnovers, limited the Panthers to 12 first downs and never let them venture past the Green Bay 35 after Kasay's 23-yard field goal closed out the Carolina scoring with 3:23 to play in the third quarter.

Kasay's kick following a 32-yard effort by Jacke made it a 20-13 game, but then Levens gained 66 yards on a screen pass, and Bennett scored from the 4 with 1:58 left in the third quarter. When Jacke got his third field goal 4:58 into the final period, the road to the Super Bowl was clear, and the post-game party was almost ready to begin.

"The excitement was unbelievable, just winning the game and then finally getting into the locker room and celebrating with your teammates," said center Frank Winters. "There weren't a bunch of fans on the field, but when they put the podium up and presented the trophy to the NFC winning team I remember looking down and seeing more than coaches and players."

There was a general manager for one thing. It was hard to tell if Ron Wolf was the most excited man on the field, or whether that distinction belonged to Packer President Bob Harlan. Both of them have described the victory over the Panthers as their greatest moment at Lambeau Field.

Wolf pumped both arms in the air in the closing seconds of the game, and then he gestured to the crowd during the presentation ceremony. He made another more important gesture afterwards when he said he planned to sign a contract extension. There had been rumors that New England and the New York Jets were willing to offer him an ownership role. But after what had happened on the field that Sunday, Wolf didn't show much interest in going anywhere.

"It was a very, very special day for me," he recalled. "I spent 41 years in the game, and in all my experiences in that time that was the highlight right there. It was the highlight for me because everyone said that something like this could never occur again in a place like Green Bay, Wisconsin. The fact that it did and the thrill of all that ... nothing in my career surpassed that."

Wolf includes winning the Super Bowl in that assessment, and it's a sentiment he shares with Favre.

"You know, you're looking for people to hug, and I was up there pinching Terry Bradshaw in the butt and thinking, 'Man this is pretty cool,'" Favre said. "I don't think you have that at the Super Bowl because that closeness is taken away. The Super Bowl is more of a circus than that week was. All we kept saying the previous three, four, five years was 'If we can just get this championship game at our place, we can do it no matter who we play.'

"When I think back to that year and go, 'Okay, what comes to mind?' I probably think more of the championship game. When you think of all the extracurricular activities, you obviously think of the Super Bowl. But when I think of what about that year stands out, the Super Bowl itself was almost anti-climactic."

As anti-climaxes go, the Packers certainly made the most of Super Bowl XXXI, beating the New England Patriots, 35-21. The Panthers, meanwhile, were headed in a different direction. They finished the next season 7-9, and they were 4-12 the year after that. This was the game that started their temporary slide, and it's one they'd prefer to forget. The Packers, on the other hand, will always cherish it.

"It was just surreal," said Jacke. "There were a lot of memories walking off that field that day."

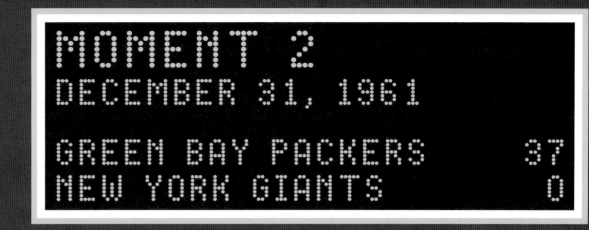

MOMENT 2
DECEMBER 31, 1961

GREEN BAY PACKERS   37
NEW YORK GIANTS   0

TITLETOWN IS BORN

One by one they left the field to standing ovations, their services no longer required. Ron Kramer, Paul Hornung, Jim Taylor, Bart Starr. Pulling his starters individually was Vince Lombardi's final payment to the troops, the $5,195 winner's share in the world championship game hardly covering the subject. These Packers had been cheered all season, but now they were adored.

So much was expected, so much more delivered. Of course, the Packers were required to send the big city Giants home muttering about hicks and Midwestern winters. But 37-0? In an act of self-fulfilling prophecy earlier that month, a group of local businessmen had declared Green Bay "Titletown USA," and on December 23 they'd held a Christmas party/pep rally attended by 3,500 citizens to legitimize the claim.

It ain't bragging if you can back it up, and the Packers accomplished that by halftime. A 24-point second quarter turned the rest of New Year's Eve afternoon into arithmetic. It could be argued that not since Chicago had obliterated Washington, 73-0, had a championship caliber team been as humiliated as the Giants. After an initial exchange of punts, they were never a party to the argument.

They didn't know where to go or what to do or even what to wear. Fearing a frozen field, some of them tried tennis shoes. The Packers, on the other hand, appeared to be wearing winged cleats.

As recently as three seasons earlier, no one would have thought this possible. Before the arrival of Lombardi in 1959, the franchise had gone 15 years without a championship and 11 years in a row without a winning record. It had to hold an intra-squad game on Thanksgiving Day in 1949 to make payroll, and it sold stock a year later to keep the doors open. Throughout the early 1950s, people in the league were talking about moving or even folding the Packers. When they went 1-10-1 under Scooter McLean in 1958, they had become the laughingstock of the league.

But Lombardi led them to a 7-5 record in his first year, and he had them playing for the NFL title in Philadelphia the following season. Minutes after they lost, 17-13, to the Eagles, he prepared the ground for what would become the first championship game ever played in Green Bay.

"We went into the Philadelphia game a little bit young and a little bit immature as far as being ready to step up and win the whole thing," recalled Boyd Dowler, who would catch three passes including one for a touchdown against the Giants. "We didn't play bad, but we didn't step up and make the plays we should have made, and they had older, more experienced players.

"We had guys coming into the locker room after the game upset and yelling and throwing their helmets around, but Vince came in and told us to settle down. He told us, 'You didn't win, but you're going to go home in the off-season and think about it and be ready to go because as long as I'm here, we will never, ever lose another championship game.'"

And so the Packers were ready to go the following fall. At least most of them were. But Uncle Sam had other plans for Hornung, who was in the army reserves, and for Dowler and Ray Nitschke, who were in the National Guard. They were all called into active duty, and the Berlin crisis had become a Packer crisis. Nitschke and Dowler headed off to Fort Lewis, and Hornung reported to Fort Riley over a three-week period in November.

It could have been worse. Playing on weekend passes, Hornung and Nitschke missed only two games apiece, and Dowler made them all, but it wasn't a sure thing that Hornung would be on hand to play the Giants. David Maraniss writes in his book *When Pride Still Matters* that Lombardi had to make a personal appeal to President John F. Kennedy to get him an early furlough.

If there had been an election in the two weeks between the regular season and the championship game, Kennedy might have carried Brown County in a landslide. Instead, there was a cold snap. The temperature plunged to 15 below zero in the days

Starting cornerbacks Hank Gremminger (top) and Jesse Whittenton each intercepted Y.A. Tittle passes. Whittenton was the game's defensive standout, holding Del Shofner to three catches for 41 yards.

leading up to the game, making it impossible for the Packers to get much done in practice. But then the mercury rose in time for the kick-off. The Packers were used to the fickle Wisconsin winters. The Giants weren't.

"They got confused when it was so cold earlier that week," said Kramer. "We had practiced for two weeks, and the warmest day was like 5 below. It was 19 or 20 degrees on game day, which was like summertime for that week. They came out, and they were trying this and that. They tried tennis shoes, but we wore our cleats, and they worked better. They were just confused."

And maybe a little outmanned. The men who played on the '61 Packers can't seem to make up their minds whether it was the best Green

Willie Wood breaks up a pass intended for Joe Walton.

Bay team ever, but they all agree it was awfully good. Hornung was the league's Most Valuable Player that year, and eight other Packers made the Pro Bowl. What's more, the chemistry in the locker room was as productive as the personnel on the field.

"The most import thing on a Lombardi team wasn't individual performance," Kramer said. "Everybody performed — the whole team. If you look at that game, everybody performed at their peak in order to win 37-0. Everybody knew what everybody else was doing. We lived together, we laughed together, we played together. We did everything together. We still do."

The living together part may have had its drawbacks. Hornung recalled that Kramer and he resided with Max McGee, an explosive combination if ever there was one. Hornung seemed to remember a friend staying up and drinking with Kramer all night before the game. Kramer offers a different version of the story, but it seems safe to say that the tight end was not tucked safely into his bed before the evening news.

"When I got up that morning, Kramer smelled like a brewery," Hornung said. "I said, 'What are you doing?' and he said, 'Don't worry about it. We'll kick their tails.' I told him if he came close to Lombardi, Lombardi would kill him. Then he wore one of those rubber jackets. I think that was the game where he got into the huddle, and Bart had to back away from him. He smelled unbelievable. He reeked. But he was phenomenal."

Kramer basically disputed everything but the "phenomenal" part. He didn't even agree on who the roommates were, substituting cornerback Jesse Whittenton for McGee.

"We went out to dinner, and I was home by 11 o'clock," he said. "I had my wife there and my newborn child. I didn't do much the night before the game. We always had a martini or two, but there was no big deal about that. Paul and Jesse moved out of the house to let my wife move in for that week."

Kramer insisted that he's never had a hangover in his life, which Hornung took to mean he was still drunk for the kick-off. "Hell no, I wasn't," Kramer said. "If I was, I played pretty good drunk."

And on that point, there was no room for argument. An unreal athlete, Kramer had been the Most Valuable Player at the University of Michigan three times. The Detroit Pistons drafted him the same year as the Packers made him the fourth choice in the NFL draft. He was also a high jumper on the track team with 4.6-second speed in the 40-yard dash.

All of that athleticism took its toll on the Giants when he caught passes of 13 and 14 yards for touchdowns as well as a 37-yarder that set up a field goal. Not shown in the statistics were several crushing blocks that had Giants middle line-backer Sam Huff wishing he would pick on somebody his own size.

Kramer couldn't say exactly how much he weighed for that game, but he was guessing about 275 pounds, which was roughly 15 more than he'd carried through most of the season. He hadn't missed any meals in the two-week hiatus between the regular season and the game, and he was a load.

"They couldn't cover him," said Dowler. "Nobody could that year. They were playing man because nobody played much zone, and they couldn't get him off his feet. He was really good. He started getting hurt after that, but he was really, really good. With Max and I outside and him inside, we had some pretty strong guys who could run."

They had that, and of course they had Starr and Hornung. Starr completed 10 of 17 passes that day to just three receivers — Kramer, Dowler and Hornung — but three of his completions went for touchdowns. Hornung was named the game's Most Valuable Player when he tied a playoff record

Hornung lines up one of his three field goals on the way to a record-tying 19-point game.

with 19 points on a touchdown, three field goals and four extra points. The honor came with a new red Corvette from *Sport* magazine, which unfortunately was scheduled to be presented to him in New York on the Wednesday following the game. That was also the Wednesday when Hornung was due back at Fort Riley.

While the halfback clearly deserved the sports car, the Packers' defenders should have qualified for a fleet of tanks. They held the Giants to 130 total yards, including just 31 rushing and allowed them past the 50-yard line only twice. New York fumbled the ball away once, and Hall of Fame-bound quarterback Y.A. Tittle was intercepted four times while searching frantically for his favorite target. That would be Del Shofner, who had been swallowed whole by Whittenton, a Bears cast-off picked up in 1958 as a free agent.

Shofner was the league's third-leading receiver in 1961, but he didn't look like it while he was making only three catches for 41 yards and giving Whittenton some unintended assistance. "Every time he was going to run a short pattern, he'd come off the line of scrimmage waving his arm like he was really going to take off running. You know, digging hard," Whittenton said. "Then he'd break it off with a short pattern. So I never did go for his arm faking."

Little things like that went the Packers' way all day long. They did fumble one time, but that was excused by a mix-up. Starr put it on the ground, but the play was not only erased by a Packer penalty, but the officials got confused moving the sticks and wound up giving Green Bay five downs.

As if the gremlins and the manpower advantage weren't enough, the Packers also had a record crowd of 39,029 crazies on their side. "We hadn't won in how many years?" said receiver Gary Knafelc. "How could you be in Lambeau and not feel the electricity? People are right next to you. It carries over to the players."

And then there were all those people who were watching from home. Thanks to the fledgling wonder of television, this was pro football's first million dollar game with a live gate of $400,000 and a TV take of $615,000. It was over so soon, the viewers had to feel shortchanged. Virtually all of the action was packed into Green Bay's 24-point second quarter, which went like this:

Paul Hornung catches an 8-yard swing pass from Bart Starr. Two plays later, the Packers scored the game's final points on a field goal.

169

Giants punt, Hornung runs 6 yards for touchdown. Tittle intercepted, Dowler catches 13-yard pass for touchdown. Tittle intercepted, Kramer catches 14-yard pass for touchdown. Giants stall on Packers' 6, Hornung kicks 17-yard field goal. Halftime score 24-0. Game over.

"We ran the ball and threw the ball, they fumbled and threw interceptions" is the way Dowler summarized it. "We just kind of blew it open. We scored three touchdowns so fast it was scary."

The Packers would add Kramer's second touchdown catch and Hornung's second and third field goals before Lombardi began to empty his bench and the customers began to empty the stands. The field announcer told the fans to leave the goal posts alone, which was like demanding that they send the Giants sympathy cards. The four-inch steel pipe standards fell like saplings, and parts of them were later found being dragged behind a station wagon in downtown Green Bay.

Knafelc recalled that Lombardi wouldn't allow the players to participate in the on-field celebration because he didn't want any problems with fans. "He told us, 'When the game is over, get in the locker room,'" Knafelc said.

Some of them seemed to be wishing the game would never be over. "I was mad at Lombardi that we didn't win 77-0," said Hornung. "It was 30-0, and he called off the dogs. I told him, 'Put us back in. We want to score 60 points.' He told me to go sit down. Of course, he was good friends with the Mara family. He didn't want to embarrass them. But I did. That's the only game that I ever wanted to do that."

The faithful weren't so greedy. They thought 37-0 was plenty of reason for a party. They flooded downtown in cars and on foot. It was New Year's Eve, and the bars were open until 3 a.m. Why not get an early start? "Cruising" wasn't in vogue yet, but there were convertibles with their tops down in December and sedans filled with as many as 15 people providing a preview. Twenty-two accidents and an undisclosed number of arrests didn't put much of a damper on the celebration.

President Kennedy sent a congratulatory telegram to Lombardi. Teams weren't going to the White House yet. Instead, Lombardi went to the league meetings. Then he and his wife went on a celebratory vacation. Not the Disneyland type, though. They chose Italy.

Disneyland was old stuff. Titletown was brand new.

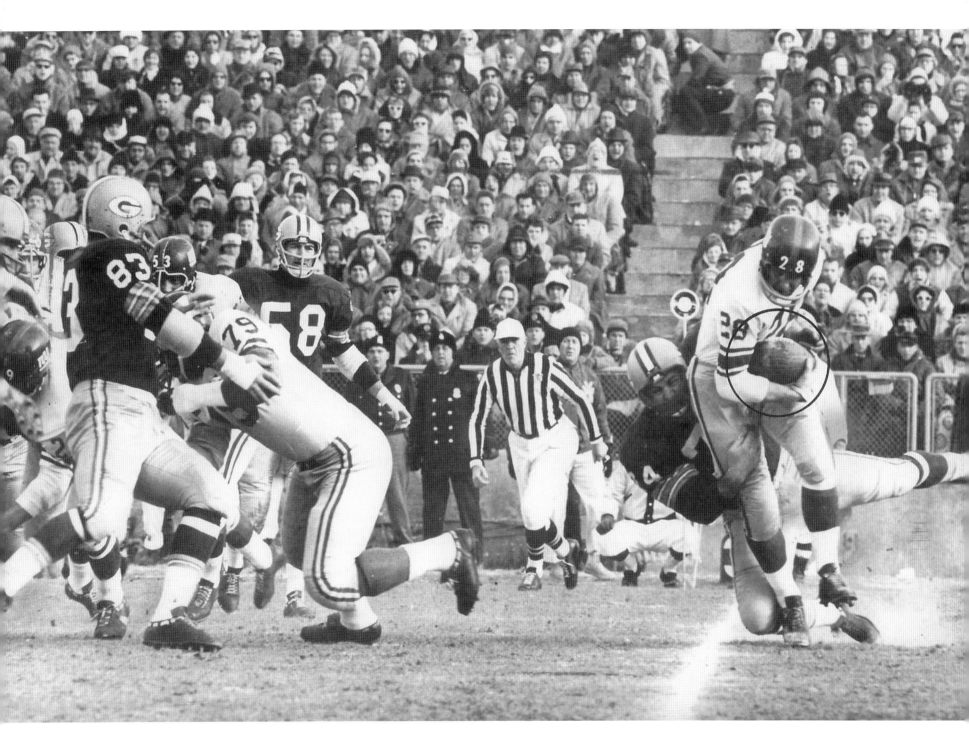

Henry Jordan nails the Giants' Joel Wells after a one-yard gain on the game's first play.

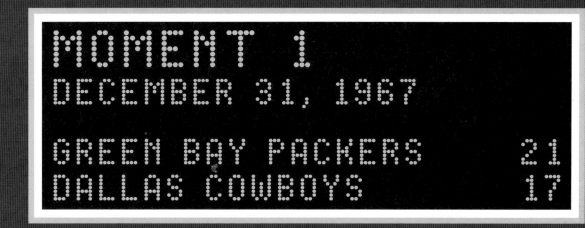

```
MOMENT 1
DECEMBER 31, 1967

GREEN BAY PACKERS        21
DALLAS COWBOYS           17
```

SECRETS OF THE ICE BOWL

The quarterback and the coach were every bit as frozen as the field. Sixteen seconds remained in the NFL championship game, and Bart Starr was spending the Packers' last timeout in teeth chattering conversation with Vince Lombardi. Starr had a surprise in mind, not only for the Dallas Cowboys, but for his own teammates.

The electric blanket the Packers had installed beneath the sod for just these occasions had been overwhelmed by the minus–46 degree wind chill, and the shadow cast by the scoreboard had turned the field into glare ice, especially at the south end. This was Lambeau Field, but it could have been the rink at Rockefeller Center. On Green Bay's next-to-last play Starr had handed off to Donny Anderson, who slipped as he took the ball and barely made his way to the line of scrimmage without putting it on the ground.

That was way too close for Starr's comfort as he discussed third and goal with the boss. Lombardi wasn't interested in a field goal; the Packers were going for the end zone. The only question was how to get there. The answer was something called "Brown right 31 wedge" but with a twist that no one except Starr and Lombardi knew was coming.

The play called for the fullback to drive to the hole between the center and right guard, with Ken Bowman and Jerry Kramer double teaming Dallas' Jethro Pugh. Pugh stood 6-6 and tended to play a little high.

The fullback was Chuck Mercein, and who would ever have figured that? The Packers had acquired the Milwaukee native when Jim Grabowski went down with a knee injury with six games left in the regular season. Mercein had played semi-pro ball for Westchester in the Atlantic Coast Football League earlier that season, after being cut by the Giants, and

A sellout crowd of 50,861 endures 13 below temperatures.

Jethro Pugh, Cornell Green and Mike Gaechter (left to right) seek shelter on the Cowboys' bench.

he had played only sparingly until the playoffs.

A Yale graduate, he was bright enough to recognize an opportunity when he saw one. He had gained two first downs and 34 of the 67 yards that the Packers covered in their final drive to the Dallas 1. He was already a hero, and a touchdown could make him a saint.

But Starr had other ideas.

"The backs couldn't get their footing, so when I took the final timeout, I asked the linemen if they could get their footing for one more wedge play," he recalled. "That was our lead play on short yardage. Jethro Pugh's height when he came off the charge was part of it. So when I went to the sideline, I said, 'Coach, there's nothing wrong with the play, but the backs can't get to the line of scrimmage. They're slipping and sliding.'

"The field just became harder and harder. So I said, 'I'm upright. I can just shuffle my feet and lunge in.' All he said in the cold and at a crucial time in the game was, 'Then run it and let's get the hell out of here.' Those were his exact words, and I'm chuckling as I run back to the huddle."

When he got there, he declined to let anyone else in on the joke. Maybe he was afraid his teammates would fall over from the shock of him calling a quarterback sneak, a play Starr ran about as often as Lombardi cracked jokes on the side-

Chuck Mercein finds a hole and picks up 7 yards on the second play of the winning drive.

Donny Anderson slips and barely holds onto the ball as he makes it back to the line of scrimmage on the play prior to the winning touchdown.

line. But Starr said there wasn't any particular reason to tell his colleagues what he was up to. "No, you just call '31 wedge,'" he said. "I just kept it and ran in."

It all sounds so logical now, but Mercein admits he was very surprised when he saw Starr carrying the ball.

"We didn't even have a quarterback sneak in our repertoire," he said. "I don't remember Bart Starr running another sneak the whole time I was there. But we had just had a nearly disastrous play on the dive to Donny when he slipped on the ice and was almost prone to the ground when he took the handoff. No one knew when Bart came back into the huddle that I wasn't going to get the ball, including me. I took off thinking I was going to get the ball.

"I had a good take-off. I didn't slip. I was practically there in two steps. I'm almost in the hole when I realize I'm not going to get the ball, that he's going to keep it. So the next thing I thought was 'Pull up. Don't push him into the end zone or assist him, which is a penalty.' I couldn't stop. So that was when I threw my hands up in the air to kind of indicate to the officials, if they thought I was trying to push him in, that I didn't have anything to do with it."

There was no flag. Pugh went down. Starr went in and the Packers were 13 seconds from successfully defending their NFL title. But exactly how both of those players got where they were is still a matter of opinion. Widely divergent opinion. The debate over who did what on the block that freed Starr hasn't been settled yet. The debaters are Kramer and Bowman.

Mercein's version supports Bowman. "It wasn't only a Jerry Kramer block," he said. "It was both people blocking, Ken Bowman and Jerry. If you look at the films, Jerry got a tremendous, tremendous jump. He got into Jethro Pugh real good and drove him pretty good. But Ken finished it off. It was a double effort."

It's Kramer's effort, though, that tends to get most of the credit. He had turned the block into a cottage industry, and it was a perfect ending to the diary he kept that season for the book *Instant Replay*.

Ask Bowman how big a part he had in the play, and he says, "Well, if you talk to Jerry Kramer, probably not too. I think in one of his many books, Kramer claimed credit for the block, but I think if you get hold of Jethro, he'll tell you that it was a double-team. I credited Jerry Kramer all these years with hitting him and standing him up, but Jethro will tell you he was pass rushing because that was the only thing that made any sense to him. That at any rate is what Jethro told me 10 or 12 years ago at a golf outing.

"Actually, I think Jerry hit him in the left hip and slid off. I always credited him with standing him up because I got into Jethro's right rib cage. You almost can't see me. He's draped over me, and I'm in his right rib cage, and I kind of pushed him back into the end zone. Basically, my biggest problem was that I didn't realize what a franchise play that was going to end up being. I told Jerry on his way to the podium, 'Don't forget to tell them it was a double-team.' He said, 'Oh, you've got another 10 years to make another block. Give me my day.' And he walked up and took all the credit."

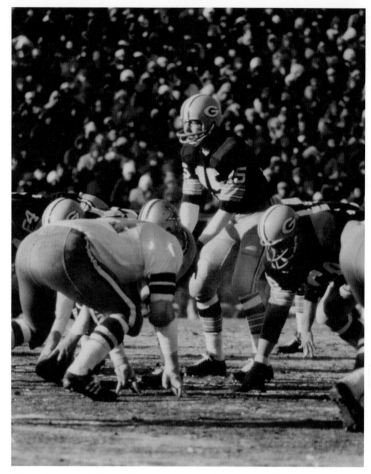

Quarterback Bart Starr takes the snap. Starr completed 14 of 24 passes for 191 yards and two touchdowns in brutal conditions.

When Kramer's asked how much credit should go to Bowman, he says, "As much as he deserves." Which may be another way of saying, not much. From Kramer's point of view, the type of block required to move Pugh was not exactly Bowman's forte.

"Look at Kenny's history," he said. "Look at the kind of drive blocks Kenny had over his career. Look at how powerful he was at driving people off the ball and then come back and ask me that question.

"I think he could have gone and gotten a program or a hot dog, and it wouldn't have made a damn bit of difference. I really don't think he assisted much on that play. I think when I got into position, the play was over. It was a foregone conclusion from that point. Kenny may or may not have been a part of it, but it really didn't matter."

While the former teammates agree to disagree on this signature moment in Packer history, there's no argument about the significance of the game or the conditions under which it was played. It was huge. And it was cold.

By beating the Cowboys the Packers became the first team to win three straight championships since the NFL introduced post-season play in 1933. They had won three in a row from 1929 to 1931, but in those days the title was determined by the final standings. The road to the throne was longer in 1967 when the NFL split into four divisions, with the division winners qualifying for the playoffs. Green Bay had to beat the Los Angles Rams at Milwaukee County Stadium to earn its date with Dallas, while the Cowboys were routing the Cleveland Browns.

The Packers were underdogs in their 28-7 victory over the Rams because many observers considered them to be a team on the decline. Paul Hornung had retired after being taken in the expansion draft, while Jim Taylor had signed with the New Orleans Saints, and their replacements both went down for the season in a 13-10 loss to Baltimore in Game 8. Elijah Pitts ruptured his Achilles tendon in that game, and Grabowski tore up his knee.

So as the Cowboys came to town seeking revenge for their 34-27 loss to Green Bay in the 1966 title match, the Packers looked anything but invincible. But there was no questioning their motivation.

"Everybody knew the week before we stepped on the field that this was it," recalled linebacker Dave Robinson.

"This was Vince's chance to win three consecutive championships. We knew the odds were that the team that won that game was going to win the Super Bowl. We knew this was the one thing Vince always wanted: three consecutive championships."

What nobody wanted was to play in conditions best suited to sea lions, but that's what the two teams got that day. The temperature at kickoff was 13 below zero, and it was expected to drop to 20 below when the sun went down. The UW-La Crosse marching band's halftime show was canceled when 11 of the musicians had to be taken to the hospital after practicing on the field earlier in the morning. The Packer Band managed to play a little in the first half, but then the instruments froze.

The grounds crew built a tent over each bench using plastic, canvas and pipe and leaving only the front open. Eight space heaters putting out 320,000 BTUs an hour were fired up, with three aimed at each bench and two at the band and the Packer Golden Girls. According to place-kicker Don Chandler, they weren't nearly enough.

"We wore our hoods and things, and they had some propane burners on the side, but there was no way you could stay warm," Chandler said. "The capes we had were more for rain than warmth. They were better than nothing, but it's just not the kind of weather where you want to play football. It was brutal. Kicking was awful. It was like kicking a wall."

It may have been even worse for the fans. There were 50,861 of them, and they came dressed for a deer hunt. Or a bank robbery. Many of them had their faces covered with ski masks or surgical masks. By halftime they had lost all touch with their feet, even though some were wearing up to six pair of socks. It was a day when survival trumped patriotism as most people kept their hats on when the National Anthem was played. Sixteen spectators would be treated at St. Mary's Hospital that evening for frostbite.

The players could feel their pain. "That was the coldest I've ever been in my life," Robinson said. "At halftime, the field just had a crust on it. You could break through the crust and get down to some dirt, but by the time the game ended, it was a solid, frozen field."

Even the television team shared in the misery. Ray Scott insisted on keeping the window open in the CBS booth, and Packer historian Lee Remmel remembered Frank Gifford setting a cup of coffee down on the counter behind him and finding it frozen solid when he went to take a sip a couple of minutes later.

This was way beyond Packer weather, but it did have its advantages for the team from the north. Most of the Cowboys had never seen anything close to this, and it showed in strange ways.

"It was cold for both teams, but we were more used to it," Bowman said. "Herb Adderley says it was a piece of cake covering Bob Hayes because every time Hayes was the primary receiver on a play, he'd take his hands out of his pants. The rest of the time when he wasn't the prime receiver, his hands would be inside his pants or a little pocket warmer in the front of his jersey."

Hayes would catch three passes in the game, but for a total of only 16 yards. This was not a day for offense, although the Packers did generate enough of it to take a 14-0 lead on touchdown passes of 8 and 46 yards from Starr to Boyd Dowler.

"They screwed up the defense in

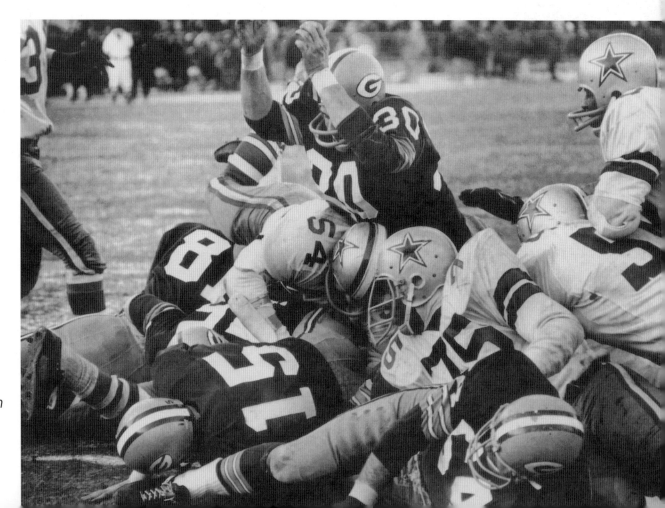

Bart Starr scores the winning touchdown behind blocks by Jerry Kramer (64) and Ken Bowman (not pictured). Chuck Mercein (30) lands on top of the pile.

The south goal posts are no match for the fans celebrating the Ice Bowl victory.

both cases," Dowler said. "I just had to run. The first one was a little quick post on an audible by Bart which we had never, ever run from that formation. I was lined up at the weak side tight end position, and he saw the guy (cornerback Mike Johnson) playing me outside, and all I had to do was release inside and break over the middle. The guy was beat before the snap.

"The long one was a play-action pass. I think Johnson and the safety, Mel Renfro, both bit on the run fake. I didn't do much to beat either one of them. Bart threw it, and I caught it. It wasn't like any work of art for me."

Meanwhile, the Cowboys' offense was getting nothing done, but their defense hauled them back into the game when Willie Townes hit Starr, who fumbled the ball to George Andrie, who ran it 7 yards into the end zone. The quarterback, who was sacked 8 times for 76 yards in losses, wasn't the only Packer having trouble holding onto the ball. Dallas punted on its next possession, and Willie Wood fumbled to the Cowboys on the Green Bay 17, setting up a field goal that cut the lead to 14-10 at halftime.

"We got into some pass protection problems and stopped moving the ball," Dowler said. "They made one play on offense all day. Dan Reeves threw that pass to Lance Rentzel, and they scored. Otherwise, their offense did almost nothing. We gave them 10 points, and they scored 17."

Those last 7 came on a halfback option pass from Reeves to Rentzel that covered 50 yards eight seconds into the fourth quarter, and for a very long time it looked as if it would be enough to win the game. The Packers took over on their 32 yard line with 5:04 remaining after a Dallas punt and needed nine plays and 4 minutes and 34 seconds to get to the Cowboys' one. "I think we drew on everything we had ever done as a team on that drive," Dowler said. "Bart just came out there and looked at everybody and said, 'We're taking this down the field.'"

Starr started the drive with a 6-yard pass to Anderson, and then Mercein ran for 7 and a first down. "That got me all juiced," Mercein said. "It was right at our bench and right at Lombardi. He was all excited. He said, 'Thata boy, Chuck. Way to go.' It just really picked up my spirits and made me feel like I was contributing."

Mercein had much more to contribute. The march almost bogged down as Townes nailed Anderson for a 9-yard loss when Mercein said he missed his block. But Mercein redeemed himself two plays later with a 19-yard catch that gave the Packers a first down on the Dallas 11.

"That was unusual in that I called it myself," he said. "Bart was like coach Lombardi on the field. You wouldn't talk back or suggest something to him, but I thought it was important to tell him that I was open in the left flat if he needed me. The two linebackers were taking straight drops, and they weren't paying attention to the two backs. Donny had a couple of nice catches going to his right, so I knew I could make that play if I got the ball."

Mercein barely had time to catch his breath before his number was called again on a trap play that gained 8 yards to the Dallas 3. Starr had been saving the play all day, and its success came at the expense of Cowboys all-pro tackle Bob Lilly, who read sweep and bit on the trap. Mercein said the Packers had run the sweep a couple of times during the game and had no success in blocking Lilly.

"The play was there if they just gave me the ball and nobody blocked Lilly," he said. "Lilly took himself out of the play by following the left guard down the line of scrimmage. I took the ball and ran right up the middle. It was very smart of Bart to save the play because it's not going to work more than once. Bart says it's the best call he ever made in his career."

It might have been, but he made a far more famous one four plays later. Anderson ran two yards for a first down, and then he was stopped twice for no gain. All that was left was Starr's fateful quarterback sneak for the winning touchdown.

Chandler kicked the extra point, and then he drove the ensuing kickoff into the end zone. The Cowboys threw two incomplete passes, and the fans swarmed onto the field and tore down both goal posts. It was the warmest they'd been all day.

Two weeks later, the Green Bay Packers easily beat the Oakland Raiders, 33-14, in Super Bowl II. The game was played in Miami, Florida. The temperature was 68 degrees.

BIBLIOGRAPHY

Carolina Panthers, 1996 & 2006 media guides
Chicago Bears, 1990-2000 media guides
Denver Broncos 1993 Media Guide
Detroit Lions 1994 Media Guide
Green and Golden Moments: Bob Harlan and the Green Bay Packers, by Bob Harlan with Dale Hofmann
Green Bay Packers 2006 Media Guide
Green Bay Packers 1962 Yearbook
Green Bay Packers 1963 Yearbook
Green Bay Packers 1966 Yearbook
Green Bay Packers 1968 Yearbook
Green Bay Press-Gazette, 1956-'57, 1959, 1961-'62, 1965-'68, 1972, 1979-'80, 1983, 1985, 1989, 1995
Milwaukee Journal, 1962, 1966, 1992-'94
Milwaukee Journal Sentinel, 1995-'97, 2000, 2004
Mudbaths & Bloodbaths: The Inside Story of the Bears-Packers Rivalry, by Gary D'Amato and Cliff Christl
National Football League official game summaries, 1959, 1961, 1962, 1965-'66, 1972, 1979, 1980, 1983, 1989, 1992-'97, 2000, 2004
New England Patriots 1979 Media Guide
Packer Legends in Facts: The Green Bay Packers, 1921-1991, by Eric Goska
Pittsburgh Steelers 1995 Media Guide
Run to Daylight, by Vince Lombardi with W.C. Heinz
Seattle Seahawks, 1999 & 2003 media guides
Sports Illustrated, Jan. 10, 1966 & Jan. 12, 2004
Total Football: The Official Encyclopedia of the National Football League, Vol. I
Total Packers: The Official Encyclopedia of the Green Bay Packers
Washington Redskins, 1983 & '84 media guides
When Pride Still Mattered: A Life of Vince Lombardi, by David Maraniss
2006 NFL Record & Fact Book

Photos courtesy of Getty Images (pgs. 56, 74, 84, 170),
Jim and Vernon Biever (pgs. 14, 17, 19, 20, 26, 28, 38, 41, 48, 52, 53, 57, 59, 62, 63, 65, 70, 72, 75, 77, 80, 81, 83, 86, 87, 88, 106, 108, 111, 128, 131, 133, 134, 141, 142, 153, 156, 158, 159, 162, 165, 172, 173),
Associated Press (pgs. 50, 51, 92, 94, 95, 96, 98, 99, 109, 117, 122),
Green Bay Press-Gazette (pgs. 100, 103, 104, 105),
Milwaukee Journal Sentinel (pgs. 23, 25, 31, 36, 39, 54, 66, 78, 113, 114, 130, 160),
Tom Pigeon Collection (pgs. 16, 32, 34, 42, 44, 47, 53, 60, 68, 69, 90, 119, 120, 125, 127, 129, 136, 137, 138, 139, 148, 149, 150, 151, 155, 166, 167, 169, 174, 177),
Green Bay Packers Hall of Fame (pgs. 123,145,147,164),
Green Bay Packers (pgs. 46, 102, 116),
The Henry Lefebvre Collection of the Neville Public Museum of Brown County (pgs. 35, 144, 146),
and Richard Bills (pgs. 150, 155)

Associated with the greatest fans in the world.

Since the team's beginning, Associated Bank has been proud to partner with the Green Bay Packers and share in Lambeau's greatest moments.

Associated Bank is the Offical Bank of the Green Bay Packers and exclusive home of Packers checking.

Associated
Bank

 Official Bank of the Green Bay Packers

associatedwithsports.com

WE WERE THERE WHEN A HELMET COULD BE FOLDED.

(WHICH IS EXACTLY WHAT YOU DON'T WANT IN A HELMET.)

WELCOME TO

100

YEARS

of

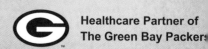